Bishop Steven G. Thompson

HE THAT HATH AN EAR

A Down-to-Earth Commentary and
Outline of the Book of Revelation

iUniverse, Inc.
Bloomington

He That Hath an Ear
A Down-to-Earth Commentary and Outline of the Book of Revelation

iUniverse books may be ordered through booksellers or by contacting:

iUniverse
1663 Liberty Drive
Bloomington, IN 47403
www.iuniverse.com
1-800-Authors (1-800-288-4677)

ISBN: 978-1-4620-1175-9 (sc)
ISBN: 978-1-4620-1176-6 (e)

Printed in the United States of America

iUniverse rev. date: 8/16/2011

TABLE OF CONTENT

THE INTRODUCTION

Foreword

Rev. Dr. Donald Ray McNeal, J.D., D. Min., Pastor, Hopewell Baptist Church of St. Louis, MO.

Mrs. Frances Whitney, Dean, Antioch District Missionary Baptist Association

A Very *Special* Book

The things which you have seen;

The things which are;

The things which shall be hereafter;

Christ and the Churches

The Introduction

The Book of Revelation has always fascinated me. Even as a child, I was lured by the *strange characters* that graced the pages of this mysterious book. I tried, to no avail, to understand the ins and outs and overwhelming facts of the book but it remained just that ... *overwhelming.*

I wanted to know more about this man, "I John" that I heard people speak of; I wanted to know John the Revelator; I wanted to know about that great number that John saw that could not be numbered; I had even told too many people that the number included us, the church. I thank God that Study has shown me that I, being a part of the church, should not be in that number, plus, there are no such persons as John the Revelator or *"I" John.*

The Bible itself was difficult enough but I was still intrigued by *this* book. Continuing to try to read, even without understanding, I only became more interested. As time progressed I learned a better way; I learned to read to know what was therein and to pray for understanding. I would never tell you that my understanding has been total, however; I am beginning, after 60 plus-years, to get a glimpse of *"what the Spirit is saying to the Church."*

I started to try to share with others as God revealed to me some of these mysteries. While shepherding a flock in my previous ministry, I had opportunity to share with that congregation. The Lord blessed tremendously and we learned together and soaked up more of the divine revelation of the book. It was such a blessing to us all that I vowed to try it again. This *commentary outline is* the results of a third attempt at a deeper revelation.

The Lord stirred me again to go forth in the book in the year 2008. I began to prepare prayerfully to take the venture. As I started, I would pass out an agenda sheet for each class. After about 3 months, God showed me "what a start I had made." He showed me that I should compile the pages that I had been teaching from and start to edit as I proceeded.

At the end of 2010, I had enough material to compile this treatise. Therefore, I must acknowledge the great family of Leonard Missionary Baptist Church for studying with me and praying for me as we made this journey through this great book. Twice each week, day and evening on Wednesdays, I had the privilege and honor to share, with these wonderful and diligent people, what God had given to me. As the Holy Spirit taught, we all learned.

With questions, suggestions and thoughts, we traveled, tried and, to a small degree, triumphed to produce this *surface-scratching* work. The *outline* is not meant to stand alone or to be read as a novel. The purpose is to co-exist alongside the Bible, the *written Word of God.* Apart from scripture this work is incoherent and of little significance.

When you have completed this outline, if you have further questions, my objective will have been accomplished. I hold that *only with clearer knowledge can one ask intelligent questions.*

With my heart, mind and soul, I thank God for allowing me this awesome privilege; serving the only true and living God and shepherding the greatest family of disciples in the world; to you LBC and *"To God be the glory"*! *It is my hope and prayer that this work will bless you as much as it did us.*

Now, come with us as we venture to "hear what the Spirit is saying to the Church."

Special thank to my wonderful wife and companion for the past thirty-four years, Lady-Elect Merlean, and to you Ms. Veronica Marshall for your keen eye and sense of appreciation for the work.

Thank You, Jesus!

FOREWORD

By

Dr. Donald Ray McNeal, J.D., D. Min.

Pastor, Hopewell Missionary Baptist Church

Attorney and Counselor at Law

Dr. Steven G. Thompson has taken the challenge to "clarify" the *Epistle of Revelation of Jesus Christ.* The journey included being faithful to scholarship and biblical precedent. He has presented Jesus Christ as the content and focus of the writing. So often, the technical merger of mystical, allegorical, numerology and prophecy entwines the author when he or she approaches the *Epistle of Revelation.* Dr. Thompson has kept the book as "confessional" for Christian believers. Words, such as "Whatever we do, our purpose in this study must be to get to know 'Jesus Christ' in a more perfect sense!" are to be commended. Each segment offered critical analysis for the reader to compare other well known writings to the content of *Revelation.*

The straightforwardness became a comfort. I have struggled over the years to find a delicate balance of being faithful to critical theological analysis and what laity already knows about certain writings. This was no easy feat for Dr. Thompson. I was refreshed to see him accomplish the same and maintain the tension throughout the entire book. Well done. The cross-references to Old Testament prophecy gives the reader a way to explore other images as they read the statements being made. I liked especially the "Author's Note" whereby Dr. Thompson came alive as a believer who respects Christ and the kingdom of God. Modern scholarship has lost this faithful confessional worship on the edge of accuracy. Also, the African American must demythologize the text to make it relevant to African American worship. This was inspiring. Dr. Brian K. Blount, Assistant Professor of New Testament at Princeton Theological Seminary recent writings in *Cultural Interpretation: Reorienting New Testament Criticism*[1] challenges every preacher, *proclaimer,* and writer to hear the content of the interpretation for Christian values. Dr. Blount considers the text grammar and concepts within the situation of the language user. It is important to take a Greek based text which has been filtered through European ideology and translation and make it relevant to African American worship. Dr. Thompson has accomplished all that Dr. Blount believes is necessary. The liberation of oppressed has not been denied for a theoretical perspective. As the text began to give detail of the epistle, there would be a welcome break in a "preacher" mode that helped the reader to anchor for a moment. Care was taken by Dr. Thompson to show the source of terms which gave the reader to do further research if desired.

---

[1]Brian K. Blount, *Cultural Interpretation: Reorienting New Testament Criticism* (Minneapolis, MN: Augsburg Fortress, 1995).

Finally, the adequacy of the writing gives laity and clergy the opportunity to complete the work without becoming frustrated. I believe Dr. Thompson has given the Church a faithful tool for further study of the *Epistle of Revelation*. I prefer to approach Revelation in a practical way rather than using the content as a fright tactic. The "mystery genre" was maintained but the *Rhema* word of God's prior revelations helped to clarify the mystery to be one that we were willing to wait to see the unraveling of the mystery. Dr. Thompson challenged the legal system on page 96 under the metaphor, "I was just doing my job." A great portion of the *Epistle of Revelation* is in "lawsuit formula." So many spiritualize Satan to the point they miss that prophetic "lawsuit genre." The writings challenged the current generational believer in their everyday walk. Dr. Thompson has kept the tradition well. It was a delight to read and contribute in a small portion to this rendering. I look forward to other works by this veteran pastor and leader.

Donald Ray McNeal

Winter 2010

Comments

By

Frances Whitney, Dean

Antioch District Congress of Christian Education

Greater Rising Star Missionary Baptist Church

Rev. Steven G. Thompson is a prolific author and speaker who gives "down to earth" information and resources for the 21st century in his Commentary on the Epistle of the Book of Revelation. The authors' notes are raving and are focused on today's life style and remind God's children how divine we are. I have never seen a better interpretation of the Word for today that is so easily read and understood.

The "Author's Points" are both convicting and edifying. To read these passages is as if you are looking in a mirror. They tell us to be heartily passionate, doctrinally sound, and zealous working for the Lord Jesus Christ, for He is *walking among his candlesticks.* The time is now to draw nearer to Him. Any failures should be confessed. All sins should be repented. All passion should be directed to Him. Are you looking in the mirror of His Word?

I am humbly grateful that I have been entrusted with and assigned the awesome task of reading and making comments on such an outstanding piece of work. Rev. Dr. Steven G. Thompson I will always cherish this opportunity that you have given me. Thank you and may God richly bless you in all your future endeavors.

Winter 2010

The Book of the Revelation of Jesus Christ

A Very Special Book

A. The Title (Revelation 1:1) ***"The <u>Revelation</u> of Jesus Christ ..."*** has as its meanings;

    a. Unveiling, revealing...Apocalypse. In today's vernacular; chaos, catastrophe; Simple definition means to uncover or make manifest.

    b. It is an Open book; God reveals His plan to His Church; the Book is a Mystery, not a problem. Problems can be solved, a mystery must be revealed. *God has not given us the bible for us to* **find** *Him but that He might* **reveal** *Himself to us."*

    c. (Hebrews 1:1, 2; 22:10).

    d. (Revelation 1:3) The Title *Revelation* is to deal with prophecy;

Jesus is the True Subject of the Prophecy! He is revealed in:

    e. (Revelation 1-3); as exalted Priest-King;

    f. (Revelation 4- 5); as Glorified Lamb of God;

    g. (Revelation 6-18) as Judge of all the earth;

    h. (Revelation 19-22); as Conquering King of Kings.

Author's Point: Whatever we gain from this study, our purpose and goal must be to get to know "Jesus Christ" in a more perfect sense!

B. The Author is *John the Apostle* (Revelation 1:1, 2, 4, 9; 22:8) ***"I, John, who am your brother ..."***who is also the

    a. Son of Zebedee and Salome

    b. Brother of James

    c. Member of Jesus' *"Inner Circle"; along with Peter and James;*

    d. writer of the Gospel of John and 1st, 2nd, 3rd Epistles of John.

Comparisons of the writings of John

Gospel of John	Epistles	Revelation
Believe, (20:31)	*be Sure, (1John 5:13)*	*be ready, (22:20)*
Life received	*Life revealed*	*Life rewarded*
Salvation	*Sanctification*	*Sovereignty*
The Prophet	*the Priest*	*the King*

A. A Book of *signs, miracles and wonders;* (Revelation 1:1) ***"and He sent and Signified..."***: *"and there appeared a great **wonder**...;* (Revelation 12:1, 3); *"And I saw another **sign"**;* (Revelation 15:1); *"And the beast was taken; ...that wrought **miracles"*** (Revelation 19: 20);

B. Why does John use *symbolisms?*

    1. *Spiritual code that is not weakened by time;*

    2. *Imparts values and arouses emotions, I.E., Beast instead of dictator; Babylon the Great instead of world system, the use of the words harlot and bride;*

    3. *Biblical symbolism must always align with Biblical Revelation;*

    4. *Some symbols are explained; (Revelation 1:20; 4:5; 5:8);*

    5. *Some symbols are understood from Old Testament symbolisms; (Revelation 2:7, Gen. 2:9); (2: 27, Daniel 7:22) (Rev. 4:7, Ezek. 1:10);*

    6. *Some are left unexplained.*

    7. ***Canonicity:** must always be considered.*

*The method by which the Books of the Bible, both Old Testament and New Testament, were determined to be the authoritative works of God; penned by man; inspired by God.

C. The Readers (Revelation 1:3-4) *"**Blessed is he that readeth...**"(what is made known to every reader);*

1. *(Revelation 1:3, 14:13, 16:15, 19:9, 20:6, 22:7, 14); any believer may read and profit; to read is "**to read out loud**".*
2. *(James 1:22-25); "...whoso looks into the perfect law of liberty..."*
3. *Seven (7) Beatitudes are included in the Book of Revelation;*
   1(Rev. 1:3), 2(14:13), 3(16:15), 4(19:9), 5(20:6), 6(22:7), 7(22: 14);
4. *The number seven (7) signifies fullness and completeness;*
5. *Other sevens : (Revelation 1:12, lampstands; 1:20, stars; 5:1, Seals; 8:6, angels, trumpets; 16:1-17, bowls);*
6. *Special messages to the churches are given in chapters 2 and 3.*
7. ***Jesus,** as the exalted Head of the church, "**knows**"...;*
8. *(v.12) "**I saw seven golden {candlesticks}**"; This is not "one lampstand" with seven (7) lights but rather seven "separate" lampstands giving light to a dark world; (Philippians 2:15); (Matthew 5:14-16). The darker the day, the brighter the light of "the Church" must shine.*

Author's Point: A strong message for Pastor's and parishioners, who choose not to build a house for the Lord in crime infested or so called "bad neighborhoods; remember ... A light does its greatest work in the dark.

9. *(Rev. 2:5) "**I will come unto you quickly...**" The promise of the coming Christ must be a motivator for obedience, watchfulness and consecration. We must live each day in **expectation and anticipation**.*
10. *(Rev. 2:7) "**To him that overcomes...**" We are known as **overcomers**; being in Christ does not exempt Saints from trials, problems and adversity; but we are more than conquerors.*

D. The Dedication (Revelation 1:4-6**) "...unto Him that loved us and gave Himself for us..."**

1. Each member of the Godhead is acknowledged. However, the book is dedicated to the *Revealer, Revelator*, Jesus Christ because of:
   a. **What He has done for us...**
      i. He *"first"* Loved us;

ii. He has washed *(freed)* us from our sins;

iii. Made us a kingdom of Priest.

b. (Exodus 19:1-6; Matthew 21:43; 1Peter 2:1-10).

Beatitude: "Blessed are they that *read* and they that hear the words of this prophecy and keep those things which are written therein *for the time is at hand.*"

E. The Occasion (Revelation 1:9-18)...*"what thou seest, write in a book and send it to the seven churches..."*

This book was born out of John's profound and prolific spiritual experiences while exiled at Patmos.

1. What John Heard (vv. 9-11*)"...heard behind me a great voice, as of a trumpet";*

a. (Rev. 4:1) *"...I heard as it were a trumpet talking with me"; a trumpet like voice;* the second voice (come up here) represents, or is **symbolic** of the rapture of the church?

b. The "trumpet" is a commission to write; and

c. Send the writings to the seven (7) churches.

2. What John saw (vv. 12-16*) "...I turned to see the voice that spoke with me";*

- Vision of the **Glorified Christ;** symbols: (1:20) "...the mystery of the seven stars in my right hand ..." ; seven golden lampstands;

a. (Daniel 7:9-14) "There was given Him dominion and glory";

b. (Daniel 7:9, 13, 22) Judge-King

c. (Rev. 19:12; Heb. 4:12); His eyes see and observe all things;

d. (Rev. 1:15); His voice as the sound of many waters (Heb. 1:1-3) the brightness of His glory express the image of His person.

e. (Rev. 2:16; 19:19-21) He wields the Sword of His mouth;

f. (Rev. 1:20)He holds the stars; angels, Messengers or pastors;

g. (Matthew 17:2); His Shining countenance;

h. (Malachi 4:2; Psalm 84:11) The Sun of Righteousness;

3. What John Did (vv. 17, 18);

a. **"And when I saw Him, I fell at His (the Lord's) feet";**

> i. *Compare (John 13:23) John lay his head on Jesus' breast;*
>
> ii. *(Daniel 10:7-9) there remained no strength in me;*

- *Being in the presence of God-In Christ, should bring us to a state of awe and respect not familiarity.*
  - *(2Corinthians 5:16) we know Him no longer after the flesh;*
  - *(Daniel 10:10) hearing His voice put me in a deep sleep;*
  - *(Isaiah 6:1) He was high and lifted up.*

Author's Note: There is a dangerous absence of awe and respect in our worship experiences today. Our attire, actions and activities do not reflect the glory He deserves. We have, unfortunately, brought Christ and "His" worship down to the level of the preacher, the choir and other auxiliaries. Too many times we worship and praise Him based on how we feel about these "fallible" creatures. Jesus presents Himself in awesome glory! We should seek to maintain that awesomeness for Him in our worship. It's all about Him!

F. The Outline (Revelation 1:19)
   1. (Revelation 1) The things which you have seen;
   2. (Revelation 2, 3) The things which are;
   3. (revelation 4-22) The things which shall be hereafter.
      - *Basic summary to the book could be as follows:*
        - (Rev. 1:1) it is a Christ centered book;
        - (Rev. 22:10); It is an open book; *"Seal **not** the sayings of the prophecy…"; (Genesis 10-11)*
        - (Genesis 10-11; Rev. 17:18) It is a book filled with *symbols;*
        - (Rev. 1:3, 22:7, 10, 18, 19; 10:11) It is a book of prophecy;
        - (Rev. 1:3) It is a book of blessings; numerous uses of "amen" in the book;
        - (Rev. 1:1, 3; 22:7, 10, 12, 20; 2Peter 3:1-10) It is a relevant book; God's Word is always contemporary.
        - It is a majestic book;
        - (Rev. 10:11; 11:9; 17:15) It is a universal book;
        - (Rev. 1:8) It is a *climactic* book.

He that hath an ear, let him hear what the Spirit is saying to the Church

The Book of the Revelation of Jesus Christ

Christ and the Churches

1. (Revelation 2:9; Revelation 3:17) *"I (Jesus) know your works..."*

2. Only the head of the church knows its <u>true condition</u> and can accurately inspect and judge each. *He who accurately inspects and judges can also repair and renew.* (Revelation 2:23b) Only He can search the reins and heart;

3. *(Revelation 2:7, 11, 17, 29; 3:6, 13, and 22) what the Spirit sayeth unto the Churches...Local; Churches ... personal, individual..."He that hath an ear, let him hear...*

Author's Point: Four (4) "kinds" of churches:

1. **Admonitory Church: All churches from Pentecost to rapture;**

2. **Local Church: Church in the community;**

3. **Personal Church: The church in "you";**

4. **Prophetic Church: The church of the future; *Jew and Gentile with no divisions.***

4. *(Ezekiel 9:6; 1Peter 4:17) where Judgment begins, the church; the House of Prayer...*

A. The church at Ephesus; the Careless Church (Rev. 2:1-7)

1. **The Approval (vv. 2, 3, 6)**

ii. **A Serving Church...** they were busy doing the work in the church

iii. **A Sacrificing Church**...to "labor" is to toil to the point of exhaustion;

iv. **A Steadfast Church** ... patience, or endurance under trial;

v. **A Separated (Sanctified)** Church (2John 7-11) they were not partaker of evil deeds;

vi. (Acts 20:28-31) It is the Church of the Lord Jesus Christ *"which He has purchased with His blood"*;

vii. (1John 4:1-6) Try these spirits...*whether they are of God;*

viii. (2Corinthians 11:1-4, 12-15) lest you be deceived by one who comes preaching "another Jesus"...

ix. (Revelation 2:6) ..."*you* hate the deeds of the **Nicolaitanes '**: *"to conquer the people"; (3John 9-11);*

x. (1Peter 2:9; Revelation 1:6; Hebrews 10:19) We are a chosen generation, A royal priesthood;

xi. **A Suffering Church;** He that suffers with Christ will reign with Him;

The Accusation (v. 4)

a. *This busy, separated, sacrificing, suffering church also suffered from "heart trouble"... They had abandoned their first love.*

*Sermon: **"Where Did Our Love Go?"***

b. *(Rev. 2:2); Christ knows your positives...However... "You must have Love" and without it, you're nothing!*

c. (1Corinthians 1: 1-3) Without love (charity), works have no significance; Only what you do for Christ will last;

d. *(1Thess. 1:3)* Apostle Paul speaks of work of faith, labor of love, patience of hope; *what you do for Christ is important; why you do it is also just as important;*

e. (Jeremiah 2:1, 2) What is *first love?* **Devotion to Christ that is so often shown by new converts;** *honeymoon love; love that is not taken for granted; not routine; not relaxed; not casual;*

NOTE: Labor without love can lead to separation without adoration;

Author's Point: Labor is no substitute for love; purity is no substitute for passion; appeasing God is not pleasing God but giving God an abundance of what He doesn't want.

f. *(Rev. 2:5)* **"Remember therefore from whence you are fallen...";** They were not living up to expectations of their position in Christ;

The Admonition (vv. 5-7) *Thanks be to God, first love can be restored; Christ gives instructions for restoration;*

a. **(Rev. 2:5)** Remember or keep on remembering where you fell from; Where you left your love;

Sermon: (John 11:33, 34) "If You Want to Get Lazarus Raised, You must show Jesus where he is laid"

b. **(Rev. 2:5; 1John 1:9)) To Repent is to** ... have a change of heart, mind; resulting in a change of direction and destination;

c. **(Rev. 2:5) Repeat ... "do the first works"** of prayer, bible reading, meditation, obedient service and worship;

d. ***Lost love can lead to lost light; loss of life, loss of Christian Liberty; Invoke the "R" factor; Remember, repent, repeat.***

e. *(Rev. 2:5)* **"I will come"**...*this is relative to His coming in Judgment;*

f. *(Revelation 2:7)* **"He that hath an ear..."** *Listen, hear, and obey.*

g. *(John 3:16; 10:10) You need not perish;* God wishes that no *one* should perish but that all should come to repentance.

NOTE: God is more interested in our *repentance* than He is our "self-effort" righteousness.

h. *(Revelation 22:1-5)* **"...there shall be no more curse ..."** *This represents the heavenly state of the Church;*

He that hath an ear, let him hear what the Spirit is saying to the church

B. The Church at Smyrna; the Crowned Church (Rev. 2:8-11)

The name Smyrna means bitter *and is related to the word MYRRH. The City remains a functioning community today called Izmir. The city was persecuted for their faith. Jesus opens this treatise with His death and resurrection. Christ always identifies with us no matter what experiences we incur. He comes to us where we are.*

The Approval (v. 9); *"I know your works... tribulation...poverty; but you are rich".*

a. *(2Corinthians 6:10; 8:9); I know of your poverty: abject, absolute poverty; having nothing;*

b. *(Romans 2:17-29) The Inner man is rich and that richness is more important;*

This Church Receives "No Accusation!!!

The Admonition (vv. 10, 11) *"He that overcomes shall not be hurt of the second death";*

a. They are accused by man, but approved of God;

b. (v. 10) **..."fear none of those things";** *fear stifles, stunts and stalls;*

c. (Genesis 24:55; Acts 25:6); Ten days, *figurative...* is representative of a brief time; However, the actions will be thorough and complete;

d. (James 1:12) **"Crown of Life";** (Hebrews 12:1-3) this is the diadem of the overcomers; the victor's crown;

e. (Revelation 20:14; 21:8) Second death; this is *eternal separation from God;*

(1Peter 4:12) We must never think it *strange* for trials to come; trials come to work patience;

Author's Point: (Matthew 6:19) It is much better to be poor in Christ than to be rich in worldliness!

C. The Church at Pergamum; the Compromising Church; (Rev. 2:12-17);

a. Pergamum was known as the greatest City in Asia Minor; Its name means married; *the church is to be committed, wed to Christ;*

b. Pergamum had its first center named and dedicated to Caesar;

c. (v.13) the city was rabid with imperial cults; they are designated as **"where Satan's seat is";**

d. *(2Corinthians 11:3; Revelation 12:9) beware lest your mind be corrupted ...beware the deceiver;* The Roman Empire "bought" the church leaders by offering them wealth and riches which led to a corrupted church.

The approval (v.13) *"...you hold fast My Name; and have not denied my faith";* they are commended as they would not give their *lordship* to Caesar;

a. (Revelation 2:12) *Sharp Sword, The Word of God is a weapon; He will fight against corruption with the "Word"*

b. (Romans 2:16) *God shall judge the secrets of men by His Word;*

The Accusation (v. 14, 15) *"But I have a few things against you";* though they had positives, they were not faultless;

a. (1Peter 5:8) Beware! *your adversary, the Devil, like a roaring lion; (as in Job); going to and fro seeking whom he may devour;*

b. Compromising people had infiltrated the church; **Nicolaitanes: people oppressors; seeking to rule the people;**

c. (Revelation 2:14) the doctrine of Balaam; Lord of the people; (Numbers 22:25; 25:1-9) prostituted his prophetic gift;

Sermon: "When God Gets in Your Way"! (Numbers 22:21-25)

d. **We cannot compromise , condone or cooperate with** *(Rome), the spiritual enemy of the church;*

Author's point: Personal advancement by ungodly compromise is deadly regression.

- *"Sin; Sinning"* is the title given to spiritual fornication in this text; regardless to what the world calls it, sin is sin; all unrighteousness is sin and the soul that sins shall die.

Author's Point: Secret sin on earth is *open scandal in heaven!*

e. (2Corinthians 11:1-4); *Pergamum; married; signifying that the church (local, personal) is engaged, betrothed to Christ;*

- **Beware of spiritual adultery**

- **The church of Christ cannot afford to compromise or fraternize with the world.**

The Admonition (vv. 16, 17) *"Repent, or else…"*

a. (Hebrews 4:12) Pergamum, If they repented not, they would feel the pain of the sword of the Word;

b. (Rev. 2:12) *Christ is He who* ***"has the two edged sword";***

c. (Rev. 2:17) *(Exodus 16: 32-36; Hebrews 9:4; Revelation 2:14; Matthew 4:4; John 6:32) overcomers, overcomes;* ***He (individuals) that hath an ear;*** *I will give unto the* ***"white Stone"*** *and a* ***new name.***

This white stone symbolizes absolution from the guilt of sin, alluding to the ancient custom of giving a white stone to those acquitted on trial and a black stone to those condemned. The "New Name" is the name of adoption; adopted persons took the name of the family into which they were adopted. None can read the evidence of the adoption except himself. The *adoptee's* perseverance guarantees that he shall have both the evidence and the inheritance of "sonship."

Libronix Digital Library System

IVP Bible Background Commentary

He that hath an ear, Let him hear what the Spirit is saying to the Church

The Church at Thyatira; the Corrupted Church (Rev. 2:18-29)

Ironically, *the longest message goes to the smallest city with the smallest church. Thyatira is a military town. It boasted many trade guilds and commercial centers. Unfortunately, where these two entities come together, the recipe for corruption and immorality is served up abundantly.*

- Thyatira had an altar to the "sun god"; in contrast, Jesus introduces Himself as the "Son of God."

The Approval (v. 19) *"I know your works and charity and service and faith and your patience and your works"*; Jesus is saying...

a. You are a busy church;

b. *"Works, ...patience, and your works... we must be patient in sewing, and patient for the harvest; we must be patient enough to do the work of "evangelizing the sinner" and patient with the sinner for the word to take root in him/her;*

c. You have a sacrificial and unselfish ministry;

d. Your work is characterized by faith, love and patience; they were not guilty of mere religious activity ... which is religiosity with no reciprocity.

The Accusation (v. 20-23) ... *("you permit) that woman Jezebel, to teach and seduce..."*

- No amount of "service" can compensate for *tolerance* of evil;

a. (1Kings 16-19) the reference to the name *Jezebel, is "symbolic" of a seductive teacher; (Here we contrast the church of Ephesus with Thyatira);*

b. *God gave her space to repent and "she" repented not.*

Author's Point: Rebellion against repentance reaps reward of wrath!!!
The Admonition (v. 24-29) *"But that which you have already, hold fast till I come";*

- **The remnant: hold fast *and do not compromise* ... hold fast "till I come"; This "coming" is synonymous with the Rapture;**

   a. **(Revelation 20:4) those who endure will receive *"authority over the nations and the right to reign with Christ";***

(v.28) *"And I will give him the Morning Star";* **God's people are so closely "related" to Him that He belongs to them;**

   b. Satan is called "Lucifer" or Bright Star; Jesus presents Himself as the "Bright and Morning Star";

He that hath and ear, let him hear what the Spirit is saying to the Church

We are still listening to "hear what the Spirit is saying to the Church"! These messages from Christ to the Churches belong to the church of today just as it did in the time of writing. The message of Christ is eternally contemporary. Churches are "people"! Human nature has not changed. Therefore as we study, let us never take these letters as ancient artifacts but try to see them as ever present conditions in which we see a mirror reflection of ourselves.

The Church at Sardis; the Feeble Church (Rev. 3: 1-6)

- A very important city; A military point and Trade Center;

- An almost inaccessible plateau

   o 1500 ft. above the main road; almost impregnable;

- 50 miles East of Ephesus; 30 miles southeast of Thyatira;

- The city's main religion is after the goddess *Artemis* with its nature cults; they believed in rebirth or reincarnation after death;

    - The city was known for its manufacture of woolen garments;

"The Approval" (Revelation 3:1) *"you have a name that you live,*

If this can be called an approval, it is all Sardis received:

You have a <u>reputation</u> for being "alive"; but in name only;

The Accusation (Rev. 3:1b) *"... and are dead";*

- The "Approval" is just as quickly taken away...**BUT, you "are dead";**

- (Daniel 5:25-28) *Mene, mene, tekel, upharsin:* **"You have been weighed in the balances and** *your deeds are not found complete in the Lord".*

- They were *not fulfilling their obligations as believers.*

Author's Point: We must ever be aware of the fact that we are *saved to a purpose* **and that being to bring other "sheep" to the "Shepherd" that they too may be saved. We have been called out of darkness into His marvelous light. Therefore, we are to focus our light (***let your light so shine...***) that others may see our good works and glorify God; our light should be a beacon to guide the lost out of the darkness and show them the Light.**

The Admonition (Rev. 3:2)

- (v. 2) You (the church) must **"wake from your Spiritual slumber";** *Be watchful;*

- *Strengthen the few evidences of life that remain;*

- *Remember, Obey, and Repent,*

- (Eph. 4:4; Rev. 4:5, Rev. 5:6) *Seven Spirits of God in the Divine Oneness of the Godhead;*

- (Acts 2) *Christ birthed the Church on the Day of Pentecost;*

- *He will come on them like a thief in the night; suddenly, unexpectedly.*

Author's Point: If we always heed the Prophet, Preacher, Pastor, Christ does not come upon us as a thief. God declares He will do nothing lest He reveal it to His Prophet first. The Prophet is charged to "watch on the wall and warn the people". Hear and heed God's Messenger and nothing will catch you off your guard.

He that hath an ear, let him hear what the Spirit is saying to the Church

The Church at Philadelphia; the Faithful Church; (Rev. 3:7-13)

The City of Philadelphia was 28 miles southeast of Sardis. Its chief deity was called *Dionysus.* The city was called a Gateway to the East. Its nickname was Little Athens, meaning, *in a place of many opportunities.* The area was prone to earthquakes and was completely destroyed in A.D. 17, (Including Sardis and ten (10) other cities.

Jesus presents Himself as *"He that is Holy; He that is True, He that has the key of David";* He is holy in character, His words are holy, His actions are holy, His purposes are holy; He is set apart from everything and everybody. **Nothing is compared to Him.**

Author's Example:

For every Babe Ruth; there is a Hank Aaron;

For every Max Schmeling, there is a Rocky Marciano;

For every Larry Bird, there is a Michael Jordan;

For every Tom Brady ... there is a Drew Brees; a Mike Vick ...BUT!!!
"At the Name of Jesus...every knee should bow! He is God! There is none like Him.

1. *(Rev. 6:10) He is the True One; (He is genuine, original, authentic);*

2. *(Isaiah 15:22-25) He has the authority to open and shut doors; (Rev. 1:18) he possesses the keys;*

3. *(Acts 14:27; 1Corin. 16:9; 2Corin. 2:12; Col. 4:3) He gives opportunity for ministry;*

4. *(Acts 16:6-10) Christ determines the place of ministry;*

Author's Point: It is not up to you to determine to which church you belong! The Holy Spirit determines your ministry and place of ministry.
Profound Point: God loves you too much to leave you up to *you!*

He who holds the Key of David (Isaiah 22:22); In His holiness, He is worthy to judge the church; He that opens and no man shuts; He that shuts and no man opens. Open doors signify...work: shut doors...wait!

We must be faithful to Him and focus on opportunities and not obstacles (Faith sees opportunity; fear see obstacles!). Missed opportunity leads to missed rewards; missed rewards leads to ***ashamed in His presence.***

The fact that they had no rebukes does not mean they had no shortcomings. BUT....they had love that *covers a multitude of sin!*

(1Thess. 4:9; 1John 4:19; John 13:34; Romans 5:5) we are taught to love one another as God loves us; He loved us first; love is shed abroad in us by the Holy Ghost.

Author's Point: It is not enough, however, to love God and fellow brethren; we must also have a love and passion for a lost and dying world of unbelievers and seek to win them to Christ by the Good News of the Cross of Jesus Christ. *The Church at Philadelphia had a vision to reach a lost world and God set before them and "open door."*

The Approval (v. 8, 9)

a. (v. 8) I know your deeds, I have placed before you an **open door, opportunity for ministry as in (1Chron. 4:9, 10);** *enlarge my territory.*

b. You have a *little strength and have kept my words; you have not denied my name.*

c. *(v.9)* **"I will make them … to come and worship before your feet…"** *He will make your enemies your footstool;*

NOTE: Footstools are not only for putting your feet on but also to raise you to higher level!

Christ refers to their enemies as the synagogue of Satan: these were Jews who opposed the Christian testimony.

No Accusation!

The Admonition (v. 11)

a. Hold fast that which you have so that no man takes your crown.

The Assurance (v. 10, 12)

a. I will keep you from the hour of temptation;

b. I will make him that overcomes, a pillar in the Temple of My God;

c. I will write upon him the name and the city of My God; and I will write upon Him My New Name.

He That Hath an Ear, Let him hear what the spirit is saying to the church

The Church @Laodicea, the Foolish Church; (Rev. 3:14-22)

As the previous churches, the Lord adapted His words to something significant about the city in which the assembly is located. Laodicea is known for its wealth and for its manufacturing of an "eye salve", as well as a black glossy wool cloth. It is located near Hierapolis, known for its famous **hot water s**prings and also near Colossae, known for its **cold,** pure waters.

Author's Point: The waters were piped to the city; by the time it reached the city, the hot water from Hierapolis had *"cooled down"* **and the cold water from Colossae had warmed up; they both had become "lukewarm".**

   a. (Isaiah 65:16) *The Lord presents Himself as "the Amen", (Hebrew: truth);*

   b. (Revelation 3:14) ***"He is the faithful and true witness; the beginning of the creation of God";***

No Approval!

The Accusation (vss. 15, 16, 17)

   a. I know your works; ***"you are neither cold nor hot but lukewarm; I will spew (spue) you out of my mouth";***

   b. (Romans 12:3; Galatians 6:3*) "you" say you are rich and in need of nothing but you are wretched, and miserable, and poor, and blind, and naked. The Church of Laodicea had the problem of thinking they were something when they were nothing; in addition, they knew not!!!*

Sermon: "The Church that Made Jesus Sick"

Author's Point: Very often, people, situations or circumstance don't create problems but only reveal all ready present problems; Christ reveals the already existing problems of this *foolish church*!

The Church at Laodicea had lost

1. Their vigor (vv. 16, 17)

2. Their values (vv. 17, 18)

3. Their vision (v. 18)

The Admonition (v. 18)

    a. Buy of me gold tried in the fire, that you may be rich;

    b. Buy of me white raiment (righteousness) that you may be clothed, and your nakedness not show;

Author's Point: This is not to say that salvation (righteousness) can be bought. It has all ready been *purchased. By faith in Jesus Christ, we become the righteousness of God. "Buy" seems to give a feeling of "selling out"! Christ comes to us where we are and addresses our issues as they are.*

    c. Anoint your eyes with **eye salve** that you may see;

    d. *(As many as I love I rebuke and chasten);* be zealous and repent

The Assurance (v. 20, 21)

"Behold I stand at the door and knock; If any man hear my voice and open the door...,

Sermon: *"No door knob on the Outside."*

    a. "I will come in and sup (dine) with him and he with me";

Sermon: "Guess who's coming to Dinner?"

To him that overcomes,

    b. I will grant him to sit with me on my throne and to share in My victory;

He that hath an ear, let him hear what the Spirit is saying to the Church

Lessons for the Church

1. (Ephesians 4:4) Divine Oneness; No one of us is as (good, strong, knowledgeable) as all of us! All for one in One; The Lord Jesus Christ is the true Head of the Church;

2. (Rev. 4:5; Rev. 5:6) Christ, the Slain Lamb of God; sends the effect of the **seven (7) Spirits of God** (Isaiah 11:1, 2) *into all the Church;* **(1) Spirit of the Lord (2) Spirit of wisdom (3) Understanding (4) Counsel (5) Might (6) Knowledge (7) Fear of the Lord.**

3. (Acts 2) Seven-sevens plus one...after the Feast of First Fruits came the Day of Pentecost (50); They were in *one* place with *one* accord, **then came the Holy Ghost and the birth of the Church;**

4. (Rev. 1:20) *Christ holds the church(es) (lampstands)and stands in the midst of them; as well as the messengers, (stars) angels, Preachers, Pastors) in His right hand;*

Author's Point: The First step toward renewal or rebirth of a dying church is honest awareness that something is wrong; the first step to solving a problem is to admit that there is a problem;

5. *"Alive" carries with it the* **concept of growth, repair, reproduction and power.**

6. (Rev. 2:5, 16) Remember, Repent, Repeat; these are the three steps to renewal;

7. (Rev. 3:4) God will always retain a remnant; a *faithful* few;

Author's Note: I have come to realize that regardless to how large a congregation may be, it is the *faithful few* that actually keep the ministry moving.

He that hath an ear, let him hear what the Spirit is saying to the Church

Formula for Revival: *Wake up; be watchful; repent; Remember the Word you have received and obey it!!!*

8. (Rev. 3:5) Then shall you be clothed with *white raiment which represents the righteousness of God;*

9. (Luke 10:20; Hebrews 12:23) *Your name is written in* **permanent record** *in heaven;*

10. (Rev. 20:12-15) *A book and another book … Everyone who is born into this world their names go into the book of life.* As **unbelievers die,** their names are removed from the **Book of Life;** when all are removed; the book then becomes **"The Lambs" Book of Life!**

Author's Point: The warning here is that the church never grow *complacent and casual* lest we soon find ourselves on "death row"; If we are not mindful, we can become too casual: casual in out attire, casual in our worship, casual in our praise, casual in our attendance, casual in our love for God and one another... But thanks be to God ... No church is beyond hope as long as there is a remnant; willing to strengthen that which remains!

He that hath an ear, let him hear what the Spirit is saying to the Church

O Come, all ye faithful, joyful and triumphant. Oh come ye, O come ye to Bethlehem.

Come and behold Him; born the King of angels.

Oh, come let us adore Him; O, come let us adore Him; O, come let us adore Him; Christ, the Lord.

Sing choirs of angels, sing in exultation, sing all ye bright host of heaven above; Glory to God; all glory in the highest:

Oh, come let us adore Him; O, come let us adore Him; O, come let us adore Him; Christ, the Lord.

Frederick Oakeley
from Wade's *Cantus Diversi*

Chapters four (4) and five (5) concern themselves with *worship.* True, Spiritual worship is one of the greatest needs in the church today. There is some degree of emphasis on witnessing and working but not nearly enough is said about worship. It is not this author's intention to de-emphasize witnessing and working. However, I do believe that there should be more emphasis on worship.

Author's Point: To worship Christ is to ascribe worth to Him (Revelation 4:11; 5:12). It means to use all that we are, and all that we have to praise God. *(The value that you place in what He has done has much to do with the worship you ascribe to Him for who He is.)*

Heaven is a place of worship and God's people shall worship him throughout eternity. This is now our opportunity for practice or rehearsal! This portion of our study is a great lesson in worship and will help us to understand how to worship God and to give Him the glory and honor that He so rightly deserves!

Revelation 4 ushers us into the third part or division of God's time line! ... ***"the things which shall be hereafter".*** In this experience, John explains what shall happen to God's people when the Church Age has run its course (Matthew 28:20b).

1. *(1Corin. 15:52; 1Thess. 4:13-18) Heaven will open; there will be a voice and the sound of a trumpet; the Saints will be caught up to heaven; judgment on earth will commence.*

Author's Point: Here God gives us a glimpse into glory and permits us to hear the worshipping creatures in heaven as they praise God. Two aspects of their worship are presented here for instruction and imitation.

He that hath an ear, Let him hear what the Spirit is saying to the Church

They worship the Creator; (Revelation 4)

The keyword in this chapter is *throne:* the word is used at least fourteen (14) times. It appears forty-six (46) times in the entire book. God is on the throne and is in complete control. In this portion of the text, John emphasizes the complete sovereignty of God. With the throne as the focal point, we can easily see and understand the arrangement of the chapter.

1. **(vv. 2-3a) <u>On the throne</u>-** *Almighty God; God the father; Words cannot describe God, therefore comparisons are made; He that sat on the throne was to look upon* **as;**

   a. *(Rev. 21:11) Jasper; sardine stone, red, robed in light; (Psalm 104:2; Exodus 28:17-21);*

2. **(v. 3b) <u>Around the throne</u>** – *A Rainbow; A vertical rainbow; A complete circle; (Genesis 9:11-17); Noahic Covenant is given* **to** *Noah but not only* **for** *Noah; This rainbow denotes MERCY IN JUDGMENT BEFORE THE STORM.*

   2b. (vv. 3, 4; 6, 7) <u>Around the Throne</u>-*elders and living creatures; these worshippers are horizontal in placement; this is the King's Court;*

- *Who are the Twenty-four Elders?*

  o *(Hebrews 12:22) They are not angels for angels are never numbered;*

  o *(Rev. 1:6) these are symbolic of the "people of God" in heaven;*

  o *In (Daniel 7:9) he (Daniel) sees these thrones empty; here in Revelation, John sees them filled; possibly 12 tribes (Sons of Jacob) + 12 apostles = 24 Elders;*

  o *(Rev. 7:9) (1John 5:4,5) Robes and branches symbolizes victory; overcomers who have conquered because of their faith in Christ;*

  o *Four "beast or living creatures"; (not as in* **The Beast)** *they are nearer to God than the angels and elders; (Ezek. 1:4-14) they resemble cherubim (Rev. 4:8; Isaiah 6).*

3. *(v. 5a) (Exodus 9:23; 19:16)* **_Out of the throne_** *– storm signals; lightening, and thundering and voices; approaching storm and God's awesome power;*

- *(Psalm 9:7) God has prepared His throne for judgment;*

- *(Romans 5:21) God's grace reigns through His righteousness;*

- *(vv. 5b-6a)* **_"...seven lamps of fire burning..."; before the throne a sea of glass..."_** *seven (7) Spirits of God: completeness, totality and perfection;*

- *There is a correlation between the* **Earthly Temple and the Heavenly Sanctuary**

The Holy of Holies is comparable to the Throne of God;

The Golden candlestick is consistent with the Lamp of fire, before the throne;

The Bronze Laver compares to the Sea of glass;

The Cherubim compare to the Four (4) living Creatures;

The Priests are the same as the Elders (kings and Priest);

The Brazen Altar compares with the sacrificial Altar of (Rev. 6:9-11);

The Incense Altar is the same as the Incense Altar (Rev. 8:3-5);

And the "Ark of the Covenant" remains the Ark of the Covenant (Rev. 11);

- *(Rev. 21:22) reveals that there is no Temple in Heaven; reason being, all of Heaven is God's sanctuary;*

- *"Pure" Crystal Sea represents God's Holiness; when the sea has mingled fire, it represents God's judgment;*

- *(Ezek. 1:22; Rev. 15) The wrath of God; issued forth in His Holiness in judgment:*

- The emphasis on PRAISE is significant in that John is writing to encourage people who are under severe persecution!

Here in Chapter four (4), the theme is "Worship of God, the Creator". In Chapter five (5), the theme is "Worship of God, the Redeemer".

Author's Point: Anyone may show worship or praise to *God the Creator*; however, only those who are redeemed may worship or give praise to *God the Redeemer*. There is a vast difference in *head knowledge* and *heart relationship*. In the closing hymn, (Rev. 5:13), the praise and worship is directed to both the Creator and Redeemer.

- *(Acts 14:8) (Romans 1:25) Acknowledging the Creator is the first step to trusting the Redeemer.*

- (Genesis 1:31) Man plunged creation into sin; it is now a groaning creation;

- (Romans 8: 18-24) It will one day be a glorious creation as it was originally intended.

Sermon: *"Waiting to Exhale"*

He that hath an ear, Let him hear what the Spirit is saying to the Church

They Worship the Redeemer

Revelation Five

*The focus now shifts to the **seven sealed scroll in the hand of God.** The scroll could not be read for it was rolled up and sealed (as a Roman will) with seven seals. John could see writing on both sides of the scroll. **Nothing could be added … It was complete and final!***

    a. (Psalm 2:8) It represents *Christ's title deed* to all that the Father promised for His work at Calvary.

    b. ***A title deed could not be opened by anyone but the appointed heir; No one else is worthy!***

    c. (Hebrews 1:2) Christ is heir to all things;

    d. (Leviticus 25:23-25; Ruth; Jeremiah 32:6-15) Christ alone is our Kinsman-Redeemer; He is willing to give His life to set us free from the bondage of sin and to restore our lost inheritance;

There are three (3) requirements for the *position* of redeemer:

    1. He must be willing of own accord

    2. He must be able (have the assets);

    3. He must be a kinsman;

        a. *Other example; Boaz in the case of Ruth.*

Christ opens the book and releases the seals for He, alone, is worthy. He owns the worth (wealth);

When He removes the seals, various events begin to happen:

    a. (Revelation 8:1,2) the Seventh Seal Judgment; seven trumpet judgment

    b. The Great Day of the Lord's wrath is announced;

    c. (Revelation 11:15; 15:1) The Vial (bowl) judgment is ushered in.

Author's Note: The trumpet Judgments occur before the announcement; the bowls after the announcement.

Now, we are ready to enter the worship experience described in the rest of this chapter; we discover at least *four (4)* compelling reasons that we worship Christ.

BECAUSE OF WHO HE IS (vv. 5-7)

    a. **(Genesis 49:8-10)** *The Lion and the Lamb, we see Him in suffering and glory; from cross to crown; representative of the twofold emphasis on OT prophecy.* The Lion of the tribe of Judah;

    b. **(Isaiah 11:1, 10) He is the** Root of David, **(Matthew 22:41-46)** He brought David and David's line into existence;

    c. **(Revelation 6:16; 7:14; 19:7; 21:9)** The Lamb, God's wrath is the wrath of the Lamb; representing the work of Christ, the Redeemer;

(Genesis 22:7) (Isaac) Ask the question, (Where *is the lamb {for the sacrifice?};* (John 1:29) (John) gives the answer...Behold the Lamb...)!

    d. **(Revelation 5:12) Worthy is the Lamb!** *The description of the Lamb:*

    1. **Symbolic description; The Attributes of God;**

        a. *Seven (7) horns; perfect power; omnipotent;*

        b. *Seven (7) eyes; perfect wisdom; omniscience;*

        c. *Seven (7) Spirits; perfect presence, omnipresent.*

Christ Jesus is worthy and to be worshipped for who He is!!!

O, Come Let Us Adore Him!

THEY WORSHIP THE REDEEMER

BECAUSE OF WHERE HE IS (V. 6); *"... in the midst of the throne, and of the four beast, and in the midst of the elders";*

To begin with, Jesus is in heaven! Please be aware that He is no longer *"Mary's Lil' Baby" in a manger;* For sure He is neither *on the cross nor in the tomb.* He is ascended and exalted in heaven. **One must remember that this message is to a suffering people in dire straits and enduring times of persecution. To them, this is the ultimate message. To them, this is the ultimate encouragement!**

The savior has defeated every enemy and is seated at the *right hand* of the Father controlling all events from that glorified position. He too has suffered but God has turned His suffering into glory just as Christ will do for the saints.

Where, in Heaven, is Christ?

    a. He is "In the midst"...He is the center of all things.

        1. The four (4) living creatures

        2. The Elders

        3. The Stars

        4. The Angels; Christ is at the CENTER!

    b. He is at the throne... *glorified; No longer as He was...no longer a bleeding, suffering Lamb but a victorious, all powerful Lamb-Lion!*

BECAUSE OF WHAT HE DOES (VV. 8-10); He took the book. When the Lamb took the book (scroll), two (2) things happened:

    a. (Daniel 7:13, 14) (1) The weeping ended; (2) the praise began!

NOTE* Prayer and Praise are inseparable!!!

O Come Let Us Adore Him!

What Kind of Song did they sing?

    a. **They sang a "Worship Hymn";** *He is Worthy;*

    b. **They sang a "Gospel Hymn";** *(Thou was slain and has redeemed…);*

Heaven sings of the *redemption.* This should never be forgotten or taken for granted. We are in heaven only because of what Christ has done!
His atonement is for families as well as individuals;

In (Genesis 22) and as Paul mentions in (Galatians 2:20), Jesus is the perfect *substitute (propitiation) Ram for Isaac, the Individual;*

In (Exodus 12:3) a lamb is slain for <u>each family;</u>

In (Isaiah 53:8; John 11: 49:52); Jesus died for the Nation of Israel; the <u>individual Nation;</u>

In (John 1:29; 3:16) Jesus died for the sins of the <u>world; families;</u>

    c. They sang a *Devotional Hymn;* (1Peter 2:5-10; Hebrews 10:19-25; Romans 5:17) This also announces our position in Christ as a **Kingdom of Priests;**

    d. They sang a *Prophetic Hymn;* (Revelation 5:10; 20:1-6) We *shall* reign *with* Him on earth;

O, Come Let Us Adore Him!

In this closing burst of praise all the angels and all the heavenly beings of the universe join together to worship the *Redeemer.* John must have heard an awesome and overwhelming chorus of praises and adoration! ***O, Come Let Us Adore Him!!!*** *The hymn relates and assures us that Jesus is indeed worthy of all praises for His eternal work at Calvary.* When He (Jesus) was on the earth, these praises and worth was not ascribed to Him.

Author's Point: Jesus did not operate as the Son of God while on the earth. Purposely and necessarily, he laid aside, pulled off, poured Himself out; {GREEK, Kenosis} in His humbleness and humility. The main reason for this was a *s the "Son of God" He could not have died.*
Jesus was:

Born in weakness;

Died in weakness; however, He is raised in victory and has "all power and authority";

(2Corinthians 8:9) He became the poorest of the poor; (1Corinthians 1:24; Colossians 2:3) He was laughed at and called a fool yet now He is the *wisdom of God;*

(Galatians 3:13) He became a curse on the cross for my sake so that I might not have to bear the curse of sin and death;

They mocked Him, laughed at Him; ridiculed His attire; However, all that is changed now; He receives all glory and honor. *What a message to persecuted Saints everywhere!*

An unsaved person may praise God, the Creator, but only those who are "bought with a price" can praise God, The redeemer!

O, Come Let Us Adore Him!

"The Seals and the Sealed"

Chapters six and seven

The worship described in Revelation chapters four and five is preparation for the wrath described in Chapters 6 through 19. It may seem somewhat strange to many that worship and judgment are in such close proximity. This may be attributed to the fact that we do not fully understand the extent of the holiness of God or the true sinfulness of man; nor do we fully grasp the total picture of what God wishes to accomplish and how the forces of evil have opposed His plan.

God is long suffering, (patient), but ultimately and eventually, He must judge sin and vindicate His servants.

Some of the reports we shall be concerned with in this segment of the prophetic calendar are:

1. *(Revelation 6:9); the first three and a half years;*

2. *(Revelation 10-14) the events in the middle period;*

3. *(Revelation 10-19) the last three and a half years.*

(Daniel 9:27) An earth shaking event will take place in the "Middle" of the Tribulation Period; *THE ANTI-CHRIST WILL BE REVEALED!*

(Revelation 13:9; 16:15) Because the coming of Christ is always imminent, we must live our lives, not in fear, but on constant alert; in a state of ready-ness. In Revelation 6 and 7, John characterizes the opening day of the Tribulation as a time of **Retribution, Response and Redemption.**

LET'S TAKE A LOOK AT:

1. **Retribution (Revelation 6:1-8)**

    In this section John recorded the opening of the *first four seals;* as each seal is opened, one of the four *living creatures (beast)* summons a rider on a horse. The command is *"come and see "*but is perhaps better rendered, *"come".* These events take place on earth, in the manner that they do, because of the sovereign direction of God in heaven. **God is in control! In every situation and every circumstance, regardless to whom may be in charge, GOD IS IN CONTROL!**

    a. *(Zechariah 1:7-17) the horses represent;*

        1. *God's activity on earth;*

        2. *The forces He uses to accomplish His Divine purposes;*

        Note: God's covenant purpose will always be fulfilled

    Let us now seek to identify these horses and their riders.

THE FIRST RIDER; THE FIRST SEAL;

Anti-Christ (Rev. 6: 1, 2) **"...and behold a white horse...; he that sat on him had a bow; and a crown was given him..."**

1. **(Daniel 9:26, 27) "...a prince that shall come" who will make a covenant with Israel (Jerusalem).**

    a. *He will begin as a peacemaker;*

    b. *He will go from victory to victory;*

    c. *He will control "the whole world";*

    d. *He will turn from protector to persecutor;*

    e. *He will seek to "resemble" Christ;*

Author's Point: One of the tactics of the Anti-Christ is imitation and deception; he is called the *deceiver. Jesus is often imitated but never duplicated! THERE IS NONE LIKE HIM!*

> f. (John 5:43; 2Thessalonians 2:1-12) even the Jews will be deceived;
>
> g. (Matthew 24:24) However, the very elect cannot be fooled.
>
> h. (Revelation 6:2) the Anti-Christ wields a bow … many say the term "bow" is actually weapon-less for it does not mention arrows. However, in ancient times, with many of these weapons, the arrow was actually a part of the bow.
>
> i. (Revelation 19:15) Our Lords weapon is the *sword of the Word.*

THE SECOND RIDER, THE SECOND SEAL.

War (Rev. 6: 3, 4) "...*and there went out another horse that was red...power was given him to "take peace from the earth";*

1. Anti-Christ's conquest begins in peace. However, soon he exchanges the *empty* bow for a "sword of destruction";

   a. (Revelation 12:3; 17:3) the color **RED** is often associated with terror and death; the red dragon (12:3); the red beast (17:3);

   b. This shouts of wanton bloodshed that originated with the sin of Cain;

   c. Not only does Anti-Christ bring war but he has authority to "take away peace" from the earth; *the absence of war does not necessarily mean peace abides; just because a person does not hate you does not mean they love you; In the presence of war, anti-christ takes away peace.*

This activity parallels Matthew 24:6, 7.

NOTE* Though God is in control of this activity, He is not the cause of this activity.

"The Seals and the Sealed"

THE THIRD RIDER, THE THIRD SEAL;

Famine (Rev. 6: 5, 6) *"And I beheld and lo, a black horse…"*

    a. (Jeremiah 14:1, 2; Lamentation 5:10) the color ***black*** is often associated with famine; famine and war are very often co-hearts; the law of supply and demand. (Leviticus 26:26) ***"To eat bread by measure"*** carries with it the notion of scarcity and unavailability. The rider carries a set of balances; *the earth's food supply is government (Anti-Christ) controlled.*

    b. (Matthew 20:2) A penny (denarius) = a day's wages; a *measure* of wheat is about a quart. It will take a man a full day to earn enough to purchase a quart of wheat (about enough for him only.).

    c. *(Revelation 13:17) at the same time the **rich and famous** will enjoy plenty. The Anti-Christ will be apt to control the economy as he makes promises to feed the poorer masses.*

THE FOURTH RIDER, THE FOURTH SEAL;

Death (Rev. 6: 7, 8) *"And I looked and behold a pale horse…"*

    a. Two personages; Riding a pale horse is **death** and following with him is hell; this (hell) is *Hades, the realm of the dead.*

    b. (Revelation 1:18) Christ yet possesses the *keys of death and hell; Remember that keys represent authority;*

c. (Revelation 20:14) both these riders will be cast into the *lake that burns with fire;*

d. **(Revelation 20:13)** *Death claims the body while Hades claims the soul of the dead;*

e. *(John 11:25, 26) Saints need not be concerned by death or hell for Jesus declares the refuge of the Saints; ..."I Am the resurrection and the life; he that believes in Me, though he were dead, yet shall he live; and whomsoever lives and believes in me, shall never die."*

f. God gives Anti-Christ authority to kill one fourth (1/4th) of the earth's population; Four methods will be used:

1. The sword... violence and war;

2. Hunger... famine;

3. Death or pestilence ... disease and infection follows with war and famine;

4. Beasts... When human civilization deteriorates, nature takes over. When there is no human dominion, animals dominate. Example (Ezekiel 14:21).

As the seals are opened, Saints are relieved and encouraged to know that God is indeed in control and that His ultimate plan shall be accomplished.

The Seals and the Sealed

THE FIFTH SEAL

2. **Response (Revelation 6:9-17)** *"...I saw under the altar, the souls of them that were slain for the Word of God..."*

John records two (2) responses to the opening of the seals; one in heaven and one on earth.

THE MARTYRS (vv. 9-11) *"...slain for the Word of God and for the testimony which they held";*

a. When the OT priests presented and animal sacrifice, the *victim,* animal's blood was poured out at the base of the *brazen* altar. (Leviticus 4:7; 18;25, 30) In OT imagery (TYPOLOGY), blood represents life (Leviticus 17:11). So here in Revelation, the souls of the *martyrs, under the altar,* indicates that their lives were given *sacrificially* to and for the glory of God. (Philippians 2:17); (2Timothy 4:6).

b. (Revelation 2:13; 17:6) The Greek word *"martus",* from which we get our word *"martyr", in its simplest form means "a witness".* These saints were slain by the enemy because of their *witness* to the truth of God and the message of Jesus Christ.

c. (Revelation 19:20; 20:10; 2Thess. 2:9-12) The forces of Anti-Christ do not accept the truth, because Satan wants to deceive the people that they may believe *the lie.*

Since their murderers appear to be still on the earth, these martyrs must be from the early part of the tribulation period. However, they represent all who have laid down their lives for the cause of Christ and the truth of God. This is a true source of encouragement to all who come after (Revelation 20:4).

    d. **(**Matthew 5:10-12; 43-48) Is it right for these martyrs to pray for vengeance on their murderers? *Yes!*

Consider the fact that this is a time of Judgment and God is answering the prayers of the Saints. These are prayers for deliverance and vindication. God is judging the world and the prayer of the Saints is in the will of God. Thus, God promises to answer their prayers but that they must wait, for there are more Saints to be slain for the cause.

    e. (Psalm 74:9, 10; Psalm 79:5; Psalm 94:3, 4) There is no indecision as to whether or not judgment will fall. If there is a question, it would perhaps be, *when?* God will eventually and ultimately, without fail, judge sin. **This is not *vengeance,* but rather vindication.**

Our sacrifice is not an action of accident but rather an appointment of incident! It is God who is in control...working all things together for His plan and purpose *for the good of them that love Him.*

THE SIXTH SEAL

THE EARTH DWELLERS (VV. 12-17)

    The martyrs cried avenge us while the earth dwellers cry *hide us. The opening of the sixth seal will produce worldwide convulsions and catastrophes. This will include:*

    a. (Revelation 6:12; 11:13; 16:18, 19) Three great earthquakes!!!

        i. (Joel 2:30, 31; 3:15; Isaiah 13:9, 10; 34:2, 4) All of nature will be affected; *Sun, Moon, Stars; heaven, mountains and islands.*

b. They cry "hide us", we sing: *"Sinner man, where you going to run?"*

c. Wrath of God. (Revelation 11:18; 14:10; 16:19; 19:15)

d. Wrath of Satan (Revelation 12:17)

e. Wrath of Nations that oppose God (Revelation 11:18)

Author's Point: When men and women will not yield to the love of God, to be transformed by the grace of God, they will be subject to the wrath of God.

John's list includes kings, captains, slaves, the rich and famous, the poor and unknown; Who shall be able to stand?

The people mentioned here are impenitent; they have refused to submit to the will of God. These would rather hide from God in fear and be lost than to run to Him in faith to be saved.

f. (Revelation 16:9, 11, 21) They not only run but they also blaspheme.

In this section, let us consider some of the parallels that exist between Christ's prophetic words recorded in Matthew 24 and John's writings in Revelation six (6).

Jesus warns of a *False Christ; many shall come in My name saying I am Christ; (Matt. 24: 4, 5); John reveals this impersonator as the white Horse Rider (Rev. 6: 1, 2);*

Jesus speaks of Wars and rumors of wars; (Matt.24: 6); John reveals the Red Horse to represent war (Rev. 6:3, 4);

Jesus speaks of famines in (Matt. 24: 7a); John reveals famine as a Black horse (Rev. 6:5, 6);

In regard to death, Jesus discusses this final enemy …"many will be killed, this is the beginning of sorrows (Matt. 24:7b-8); John's Pale horse rider symbolizes … death (Rev. 6: 7, 8)

Those killed and hated for (His) name sake in (Matt. 24: 9) are the souls under the altar, slain for their testimony in (Rev.6: 9-11);

Jesus speaks of worldwide chaos, many shall be offended; shall betray one another; love shall wax cold (Matt. 24: 10-13); consistent with John's worldwide chaos; great earthquakes; sun becomes black; moon becomes blood; (all) men hid themselves in dens and rocks; … from the face of Him that sitteth on the throne (Rev. 6:12-17)

(Matthew 24:14) introduces the preaching of the gospel of the Kingdom throughout the whole world. This is where we enter into chapter SEVEN!

Redemption (Revelation 7:1-7)

Here we do a contrast of the two (2) groups of people that are being chronicled!

The comparison centers itself around Chapter 7:1-8 and Chapters 7: 9-17;

In (Rev. 7:1-8), the hosts are Jews; in (Rev. 7:9-17), those represented are Gentiles from every nation;

In the first half there are numbered 144,000; in the latter, John sees a number that could not be numbered;

The first group is sealed on earth; the second group is standing in heaven before God;

This portion also parallels Matthew 24:14

The Sealed Jews (Revelation (7:1-7) (3b) *"…Hurt not the earth…till we have sealed the servants of God…" ;*

a. Angels are significant in the judgments of God. They blew the trumpets and now angels are used in the

   i. Wind (Revelation 7:1) Used here in God's judgment on the earth, sea and green vegetation.

   ii. Fire (Revelation 14:18)

   iii. Water (Revelation 16:5)

b. (Revelation 9:4; Ephesians 1:13, 14) Seals represent possession and protection. Today the Christian is sealed by the Holy Spirit.

The sealing Angel commands the angels to hold back their judgment until the servants (144,000 Jews; 12,000 from each of the (12) tribes of Israel) are sealed. This is shown in Ezekiel 9 and also Matthew 24:31.

c. (Revelation 14:1) The Lamb stands on Mount Zion with the 144,000 that have been sealed with the Father's Name;

d. (Revelation 13:17; 14:11; 16:2; 19:20) sealed with the name of the Mark of the Beast, or the number of his name (in order to buy or sell);

e. (Revelation 7:2; Revelation 8) This seal (sealing) protects the chosen Jews;

f. (Revelation 9:1-4) The faithful are sealed and are protected from the locust that comes when the bottomless pit is opened.

g. 144,000 signify completeness and protection…12x 12,000;

The Saved Gentiles (vv. 9-17) *"… a great multitude which no man could number…"*

This great Book of Revelation gives us a **global outlook.** The emphasis is on what God does for people in the whole world.

"For God so loved the *world* that He gave His only begotten Son that *whosoever* believes in Him shall not perish but have everlasting life." (John 3:16)

  a. (Revelation 5:9) *every kindred, and tongue, and people, and nation;*

  b. Revelation 7:9) *"...all nations and kindred and people and tongues;*

  c. (Matthew 28:19, 20; Mark 16:15) ...Go into **all the world...**

  d. **These are Gentiles saved during the Tribulation; They will not be able to buy or sell for they received not the mark of the beast or his name;**

  e. Because of this, they will endure *hunger* (Revelation 7:16); (13:17) *thirst;* 16:4) *lack of shelter; (Revelation 16:8,9) heat of the sun;*

  f. These are **standing before the throne,** (not seated on thrones) to suggest that they are not the church. (v.14) reveals that they have come out of "the" Great Tribulation *"having washed their robes and made them white in the blood of the Lamb."* They are saved by faith in the Gospel of Christ, preached by the Sealed Jews.

John suggest to us at least three (3) descriptive terms for these people. They are:

  1. **Accepted:** they wear white robes and held palms symbolizing victory (Leviticus 23:40-43)

  2. *Joyful:* they sang praises and were *joined in worship by others around the throne;*

  3. **Rewarded:** they enjoy the privilege of being before God and serving Him; **"In His presence";**

They are In His Presence! (Revelation 21:4; Isaiah 49:10); they are in the presence of Our Shepherd and provider of every good and perfect gift".

The opening of the Seventh Seal will introduce the Seven Trumpet Judgment. (Revelation 8 -11) The Wrath of God will intensify and broaden. Prior to this, however, God will remember mercy (Habakkuk 3:2); many will be saved by the blood of Lamb.

At the same time, many will reject the Savior and accept the Beast and his mark.

So we bow, as we enter the throne room,

And we cast ourselves down, at Your Feet.

We sing Holy, Thou art Holy, there is none like thee.

In your presence, is where we must be!

Excerpt from "Shekinah Glory" ; Before the Throne

Prepare to blow the Trumpets!
Chapters 8 and 9

The seals judgments are now past. Preparation is now being made to *sound the trumpets.* Following the Trumpet judgment will be the Bowls judgments. This brings to a head the destruction of Babylon and the coming of Christ to the earth. There is a marked intensity from the seals to the bowls. Also note that the same areas are affected.

The Trumpets	the Judgments	the Bowls
1. 8:1-7	the earth	16:1, 2
2. 8:8, 9	the Sea	16:3
3. 8:10, 11	the Rivers	16:4-7
4. 8:12, 13	the Heavens	16:8, 9
5. 9:1, 2	mankind tormented	16:10, 11
6. 9:13-21	an Army	16:12-16
7. 11:15-19	angry nations	16:17-21

Jacob's Troubles is the title given to the *first 3 1/2 years of Tribulation;*

    Great Tribulation references the *last 3 1/2 years of Tribulation.*

This last part of the Tribulation is also called the Wrath of God (Revelation 14:10; 15:7).

The events seem to have a strong parallel to the ten (10) plagues against Egypt.

Let us now take a look at the;

Preparation (Revelation 8:1-6); Opening of THE SEVENTH SEAL

 Two factors

  a. *(Revelation 8:1) Silence; the quiet before the storm (Zechariah 2:13); from great expressions of praise to breathless sense of silence; Heaven has most recently worshipped the Father and the Lamb with a resounding praise. When the Lamb opens the 7th seal, there is **"Silence in Heaven for the space of about "half an hour".***

Most theologians think "half an hour" is only a symbolic reference to a "short space of time".

  (Zechariah 2:13) Be silent all flesh before the Lord for He is aroused from His Holy habitation.

  (Habakkuk 2:20) But the Lord is in His Holy temple; let all the earth keep silent before Him.

  b. *(Revelation 8:2-6) Supplication; we have here the altar of incense which is indicative of prayer. The prayers of God's people (Thy Kingdom come). The incense would represent the cries of **the Tribulation martyrs (Revelation 6:9-11).***

"Thunders" usually give warning that the storm is coming. The seven angels stand poised for action! Then they begin to sound...one by one! The Angels are ready; *Are you?*

        c. (Zephaniah 1:7; 14-18) (16) *A day of trumpet and alarm against the fortified cities and against the high towers.*

The trumpets are given to the angels during the Silence.

Trumpets are also significant in biblical history;

1. (Numbers 10:1-8) called the people together;

2. (Numbers 10:9) called the people to war;

3. (Numbers 10:10) announced special times;

4. (Exodus 19:16-19) Used at Mount Sinai at the giving of the law;

5. (1Kings1:34, 39) Used when kings were anointed;

6. (Joshua 6:13) Used in Joshua's conquest of Jericho.

In (Revelation 4:1, 1Thessalonians 4:13-18) the voice that summoned John to "come and see" (rapture) sounded like a trumpet.

The chilling silence is followed by "action at the altar".

NOTE: (Revelation 8:4) the prayers of the Saints ... *"Uphold Your law and vindicate Your people. This is an "Imprecatory Psalm".*

Author's Point: The prayers of God's people are involved in the judgment that He sends; (Moses prayed for the disobedient children of Israel and God withheld judgment). How many of us are alive because of the prayers of a parent or loved one?)

Author's Point: The throne of God and the altar of God are closely inter-related. The purpose of prayer is not to get our will confirmed in heaven but to get the will of God done on earth; even when it involves judgment. We must forever keep the throne of God near the altar of God!

Desolation (Revelation 8:7-13) *"…hail and fire mingled with blood…"*

The first four (4) trumpets are natural in that they affect the land; the saltwater, the freshwater, and the heavenly bodies. The fifth and sixth trumpets announce the release of <u>demonic beings… that first torment and then kill (Revelation 11:15-19).</u> The last of the trumpets will create a crisis among all the nations of the earth.

a. **Desolation on earth (v. 7)** (Exodus 9:18-26; Joel 2:30) hail and fire mingled with blood; supernatural.

b. **The target:** green vegetation, trees, grass; *"trees"* usually mean fruit trees; 1/3 of the world natural resources will be destroyed;

c. **Desolation in the seas (vv. 8, 9)** (Exodus 7:19) water is turned into blood;

d. **Desolation in the freshwater (vv. 10, 11);**

e. **Desolation in the heavens (vv. 12, 13)** not just 1/3 but the entire world; (Exodus 10:21)(Amos 5:18)

f. **(Joel 2:1, 2) God will bring judgment on His people Israel;**

g. **(Revelation 8:13)** "Woes" refer to the judgments yet to come from the three (3) remaining trumpets;

The phrase inhabitants of earth refers not only to people on the earth but also those with an earth mentality.

    h. (Philippians 3:18) Our citizenship is in heaven; love not the world;

Liberation (Revelation 9: 1-21)

Revelation 9 describes two (2) frightening armies that are liberated from the pit at the same time and are permitted to judge mankind.

1. **The Army from the Pit (1-12)** the abyss or bottomless pit; *"and there was smoke out of the pit…as from a great furnace"; (v.3)"and there came out of the smoke locusts upon the earth."*

   a. (Luke 8:31) It is also called the abode of demons;

   b. (Revelation 20:1-3) It is somewhat of a "temporary holding cell" (jail) for Satan;

   c. (Revelation 11:7; 17:8) The Anti-Christ will ascend from this pit;

   d. (Revelation 9:11) He is a *person*; a king over pit demons;

   e. (Isaiah 14:12-14) Lucifer; called brightness or morning star; (Luke 10:18) Jesus indicates that He saw Satan fall like lightening from the sky;

   f. (Matthew 13:42, 50) …"And I will cast them into a furnace of fire…"

   g. (Exodus 10:1-20) devastating swarm of locust; Real locusts do not follow a king; they destroy vegetation.

Even though a literal interpretation cannot be ruled out, (these are "supernatural" times and all things are under God's control) these are not considered to be "literal" scorpions; they do not devour vegetation. They are told to torment all unsealed people.

> h. They are commanded to do their job for 150 days or five (5) months; the usual lifespan of a "physical" locust (May – September).

(2Thess. 2:6) as Saints of God, we can appreciate that Our Lord has the keys of death and hell (Revelation 1:18) and that He exercises authority over Satan. God is in control and nothing will happen before its time nor will it be delayed.

2. **The Army from the East** (Revelation 9:13-21) *"...loose the angels which are bound in the great river Euphrates."*

It was at the golden altar of incense that the angel offered prayers of the Saints. Now a voice is heard, commanding the four (4) angels to be loosed. They are released at a precise time (the hour, the month, the day) for a specific purpose. They are told to kill and not for torment, a third part of the world's population

It is presumed that these are "evil" angels for it is not likely that "good" (holy) angels would be bound.

> a. (Revelation 9:10) *"they had tails like unto scorpions, ...stings in their tails, ...power to hurt...";*
>
> b. (v.16) *"and the number of the horsemen were* **200 million (200 thousand thousand) soldiers;**
>
> c. Is this a literal army? What message is John seeking to deliver?

The emphasis is on the horses rather than the riders! We doubt this can be compared to modern day warfare.

> d. **The power of the horses;**
>
> > 1. In their mouth and tails; not in their legs;

2. Fire, smoke and brimstone;

3. Tails like biting serpents;

4. Attack from the front as well as the rear.

e. These judgments are retributive (payback) and not remedial (correction); in this judgment, there is no room for repentance. The actions are penal not corrective.

f. (Revelation 6:9-11) This is vindication; the answer to the prayer of "how long"?

g. (Revelation 9:20, 21) **"And the rest of the men which were not killed by these plagues yet repented not…";** Even while God is judging these evil deeds, mankind still insist and persist in sin and sinning;

Author's Point: The Promise of punishment is not a deterrent to wrong doing". **Example:** *As a child, even though I knew my daddy would punish me for doing wrong, I still did what I did …*

Some of the sins mentioned by John are:

1. (1Corinthians 10:19-21) (Isaiah 14:12-15)(Matthew 4:8-10) Idolatry or demon worship; Sinners "dead" in their sin, worshipping dead gods;

2. Murder and theft; a result of money, provisions and necessities being a premium and very much in demand;

3. Sexual immorality; many times during stressful times, mankind resorts to this outlet;

During this recession (2009), a recent commentary showed that "strip joints" and sex oriented clubs (i.e., Hooter's, Hustler's) are prospering more than ever. Attendance is at an all time high. (KMOV TV)

4. **Sorcery; GREEK:** *Pharmakia; drug abuse;*

5. (Judges 21:25b) *"Everyone did what was right in his own eyes".*

God has planned a work and is now working His plan. Nothing that Satan or his army can do will ever hinder God's plan. *Prepare for other phenomenal events to occur.*

END OF TIME AND THE *TWO WITNESSES*

This chapter introduces us to the "middle" of the Tribulation period. According to (Daniel 9:27), this is the time that Anti-Christ will break his covenant with Israel and reveal his true identity. The two witnesses' minister during the first half of Tribulation and the Jewish remnant are protected during this time. The Beast (Anti-Christ) will exercise world authority during the last 31/2 years of the tribulation and will commit awful persecutions against the Believers. This is considered a "parenthetic" between the sixth and seventh trumpets (Rev.10:1- 11:14).

The seventh trumpet will introduce the seven vials of the wrath of God and "the Great Tribulation" gets underway!

1. The Appearance of the Angel (Revelation 1:1-4) ***"…and the angel stood…"***

    According to the trend of (Revelation 1:12-16), this angel is Jesus. Ascribed to His work is His power; (11:3) **"I give My power to My two (2) witnesses."**

    a. (Revelation 5:2) ***"Strong Angel";*** now John sees another Mighty angel.

    b. (Revelation 1:12-16) The Angel holds the seven stars (messengers) in His right hand; Out of His mouth went a sharp two edged sword; His countenance is as the sun; His feet as fire, this is **the glorified Christ.**

    c. (Revelation 5:5; Hosea 11:10, Joel 3:16) His voice is as that of a lion.

Here, Christ, the Angel of the Lord announces that God is prepared to work speedily and completely! No more delay!

    d. The little book is in contrast to the scroll. It is smaller. This scroll is open; the book in (5:1) is sealed. It is a book of prophecy, declared by the prophets.

NOTE* Since the prophets did not deal with the workings of the church, we say that this prophecy relates to Israel, the Jews and Jerusalem.

By standing with feet on earth and sea, the Lord lays claim to "all the earth and seas". ..."The earth is the Lord's and the fullness thereof." (Joshua 1:1-3; Psalm 24).

     e. *Can this be the fulfilling of the prophecy of Daniel 12:4- 9?*

     THE LORD IS "IN CONTROL"!

2. The Announcement from the Angel (Revelation 10:5-7) *"And the angel which I saw stand upon the earth...sware by Him that lives forever and ever... time no longer"; no more delay;*

     The "time" is answer to the Saints question, "how long, Oh Lord?!

The seventh trumpet will introduce the seven vials (bowls) of the wrath of God and the last 3 1/2 years of the wrath of God is at hand.

Be not deceived, this is not a scene of solemnity as Christ declares His Lordship... He declares that there will be no more delay. God wishes that no one should perish but that all should come to repentance (2Peter 3:9) however; the time for repentance is "before" the wrath. THIS DAY that you hear His voice, don't harden your heart. Seek Him while He yet may be found; call upon Him while He is near (Isaiah 55:6). THE TIME IS NOW!

     These things are true and sure:

       1. God is in control;

       2. God will finish what he starts;

       3. God will answer all questions and vindicate Himself as well as the Saints;

The term *mystery used here has as its meaning, "truth of God." This is not considered a problem because problems can be solved. This is a mystery in that it must be revealed.*

Author's Point: The age old "Job" question is still a mystery to mankind! Why do the righteous suffer and the evil, seemingly, go free? ; Why is there sin and suffering in the world? Be assured, God will straighten it all out and complete His plan (Revelation 11:18). In the mean time, (Psalm 37:1, 2) prevails; *"Fret not yourself because of evildoers... For they shall soon be cut down like the grass..."* **Hallelujah! Praise Him for He is worthy!**

The Appropriation of the angel (Revelation 10:8-11) ***"Go and take the little book...; and eat it up";***

It is not enough for John to see the book or even to know the contents; he must *appropriate* the book. He (we) must make it a part of the inner man.

a. (Ezekiel 2-3; Jeremiah 15:16) the command is to *eat* the book;

b. (Matthew 4:4) the word is *food;*

c. (Psalm 119:103) *"How sweet are thy words unto my tastes?"*

d. The *word* must be ingested and assimilated before it can do us any good; it must be applied, digested, memorized.

e. John ate the book and there is a dual effect;

  1. ***"and it was in my mouth sweet as honey":*** (Revelation 1:3) **blessed are they who read...;**

  2. ***"and as soon as I had eaten it, my belly was bitter";*** this is representative of the burden of the Lord' responsibility; to know is to be charged to do;

    In order to be an effective witness of the Word, one must first believe in and be convicted by the Word. You cannot effectively sell a product that you don't use and believe in.

Author's Point: Many people know the bible and can quote scripture but the Word has not permeated their spirit. It has not been *appropriated.*

f. The word *"before"* used in verse eleven would be better transliterated *"concerning"*. John would prophecy concerning many <u>nations,</u> peoples, tongues and kings.

Satan will be *stirring up* the <u>nations</u> in preparation for the Battle of Armageddon.

The Ministry of the Two Witnesses (Revelation 11:1-4)

Chapters eleven and twelve (11 & 12) bring us to another section of the "middle" of the tribulation Period. We cannot attribute or ascribe any of this to the church for it puts us in dire straits as far as canonicity is concerned. Everything that has transpired here has "Jewish" tone to it; The Temple (1, 2); Jerusalem (v.8); the ark (v. 19); the Ruling Christ (12:5); Michael (12:7); and Satan's persecution of the Jews (12:17).

A. **The Period of the Ministry (1-4)** (v.3) ***"And I will give power unto my two witnesses and they shall prophecy a thousand two hundred and three score days";*** equal to forty-two months or three and one-half years.

1. The Temple has been rebuilt and the nation is worshipping there again;

2. The witnesses have access to the Temple;

3. (2Thess.; Daniel 9:27; Matthew 24:15) Anti-Christ takes possession of the Temple; this is the "Abomination of Desolation".

4. (Ezekiel 40-41; Zechariah 2) *Measure* the Temple; or *lay claim to it;*

5. *(Zechariah 4-5) Zerubbabel and Joshua, the High Priests; Two (2) servants who reclaimed and rebuilt the Temple after Babylon captivity;*

B. The Purpose of the Ministry (Revelation 11:5,6)

1. To show or "put on display" the power of God to unbelieving Jews and Gentiles; They are called prophets as well as witnesses;

2. To announce great events that are yet to come;

3. They will incur the wrath of the Beast and the people;

4. Their powers seem to identify them with Moses and Elijah; **Another school of thought identifies them with Elijah and Enoch;**

C. The Persecution in their Ministry (Revelation 11:7-10)

1. They will be divinely protected *during* their ministry, however;

2. God then allows the Beast to oppose them and to slay them;

(Psalm 79) Their bodies will lie in the streets for (31/2) days; no burial; the world will rejoice; (Only that which is dead is to be either buried or RESURRECTED!!!)

3. Hallelujah! God raises them from the dead!

4. They are RAPTURED into heaven!

5. An earthquake will destroy a tenth of the city and 7000 men will be killed;

The Testimony of the Seventh Trumpet (Revelation 11:15-19)

This THIRD WOE was promised back in (Rev. 8:13). The seventh angel sounds the trumpet and great voices from heaven announce that the *kingdom – (singular)* of this world is in Christ's power; (the Beast has unified the kingdoms!) The Beast has been in charge, but God is in *control*!

1. This portion is *prophecy,* not present tense; The prophecy is then followed by praise; This is the third incident (event) of praise, so far;

    a. (4:10, 11) They worship/praise the Creator;

    b. (5:8-10) They worship/praise the Redeemer;

    c. Here Christ is worshipped/praised as King and Judge;

The prayers of the martyrs (*"how long...?"*) And the prayers of God's people, (*"thy Kingdom come"*) will be answered now!

Verses 18 and 19 give somewhat of an outline of what shall happen in the last (31/2) years of the tribulation called *the Great Tribulation.*

2. (Psalm 2; Psalm 83; Joel 3:9-13) There will be (*intense*) national and international hatred; Nations will show their intense hatred for Christ and His people and persecution will escalate.

3. (Rev. 12:12) *"... woe to the inhabitants of the earth..."* Satan is on the earth trying to destroy the Jews;

4. (Revelation 20:4) Here will take place the resurrection of the tribulation martyrs; and of the wicked dead (20:12). (Daniel 12:1-3) seems to indicate a resurrection of the OT Saints AFTER the tribulation;

5. In this judgment; Saints will be rewarded for their *works* and the evil are punished.

6. Even from the beginning, man has been charged to take care of the earth and to use its resources for his (*mankind's*) treasure and God's glory. Satan has led men to destroy the earth and to use it for his (mankind's) pleasure and Satan's evil.

Author's Note: Some say that the righteous have the right, today, to judge people. However, it is this author's position that we have not the right to judge one another. First, we are told (Matthew 7:1) to *"judge not…"*, Secondly, the scripture tells us (1Corinthians 4:5) "judge nothing before the time, until the Lord come…There will be a time when the Saints will sit on thrones and judge the world but the time of judgment is *"not yet".*

It is true that all sin must be judged. However, the Christian has the option to have his sin judged now and to be his own judge. (1Cor. 11:28)(1John 1:9).

For the Christian, all sin; past, present and future has been forgiven at Calvary. So why do we ask forgiveness? Since all sin has been forgiven, the asking is not for "forgiveness" *per se*, it is for the *renewing of fellowship* that is broken when we sin. *Asking forgiveness is also an act of confession. (It may be said to be like having money in the bank but you must write a check or make a withdrawal to benefit from it!)*

(Rev. 9:11) Satan is called the destroyer. The evil are here called, *"those who destroy the earth."*

The woman as Clothed with the Sun

The theme in this chapter is conflict; Conflict between the forces of evil and the people of God.

1. The Wonders in Heaven (Revelation 12:1-6)

The Woman: The Great City of Rome (Roman Catholicism) would like for the world to believe that this woman is *Mary, the mother of Jesus.* However, (vv. 6 and 13-17) makes this impossible *(canonicity).* If you read (Genesis 37:9), you can see that she represents the *Nation of Israel.*

2. The *woman,* representing Israel, **(vv. 1-5)** gives birth to *a man child,* Christ;

   a. (Romans 1:3) (Of the seed of David according to the flesh;

   b. (Isaiah 54:5; Jeremiah 3:6-10) Israel is pictured as a *woman;*

   c. (Psalm 2:9) and (Revelation 19:15) Parallels that the *woman's* child shall *rule with a rod of iron.*

Between verses five 5 and six 6, the entire Church Age takes place.

3. The *Dragon* (vv. 3, 4) Verse nine (9) makes it clear that this great red dragon, representing death and destruction, is Satan;

   a. (Rev. 13:1; 17:3) Seven heads, ten horns, seven crowns describe the Beast;

   b. (Rev. 12: 4 and Isaiah 14:12) Here seems to parallel the description of the fall of Satan to the earth, causing a third of the (angels) stars of heaven to fall to earth; Satan does have a following!

   c. (John 8:44) Satan is described as a *murderer, even from the beginning, Cain and Abel;* He did all in his power to keep Christ from being born and sought to have him killed (Matthew 2:16).

   d. (Rev. 12:6; Matthew 24:15-21) lets us see that Israel will be miraculously protected *(sealed)* during the last half of the tribulation period, which is called *"The Great Tribulation".*

These events will take place about the *mid-point* of the Tribulation Period. At this time the Beast will break his covenant with Israel and set up his image in the Temple at Jerusalem.

Let him that read also understand!

4. **The War in Heaven (Rev. 12:7-12)**

   a. We are told that Satan will have access to heaven during this age;

   b. (Zechariah 3) He is also called the accuser of the brethren;

Author's Point: Combining these two truths wouldn't it be something if Satan were present at the Judgment seat of Christ; there to behold the vindication of the Saints and to behold the beauty of (Romans 8:1)? Yes, he may accuse, but because of *"the blood", there is therefore no condemnation to them which are in Christ Jesus". Hallelujah! Praise God!!!*
The Psalmist declares…"*Thou preparest a table before me in the presence of mine enemies…"*

Author's Profound Point: The table is prepared *before me in the presence of my enemies…; the enemy must watch me feast at the table that he/she inspired. They do not get to dine!!!*

Whatever the case, Satan will be cast out of heaven at the mid-point of the tribulation; His presence is not permitted at the *marriage supper.*

   c. (Ephesians 5:24-27) all *"spots and/ or blemishes and any such things"* have been eliminated.

      1. **(1John 1:9 – 2:2) Saints of God have at least three (3) weapons to defeat Satan;**

         a. **The *blood of Jesus;***

         b. **The *Word of God;***

         c. **Their *surrender (testimony) of the will of God;***

There is joy in heaven and woe on the earth! *Satan is defeated!*

2. The Wrath on Earth (Rev. 12:13-16)

The Great Dragon comes down with intense anger. Since he is not permitted to accuse the Saints before God, he resorts to persecuting those yet on the earth. His attack is focused primarily on Israel. Satan could not kill the woman's Son, so he tries to exterminate her seed, the believing remnant of Israel.

a. (V. 14) *"woman was given two wings of a great eagle that she might fly..."* assures us that God protects the remnant;

b. (Exodus 19:4) They are delivered as *on eagle's wings;*

c. *(Deuteronomy 32:11, 12; Isaiah 40:31) As a mother eagle protects her brood;*

d. (v. 6) *" ... a place prepared of God..."* they flee to a place where *Satan cannot come;*

e. (v. 15) *" ... serpent cast out of his mouth ... "* water depicts a flood of destruction representing the multitude of Gentiles;

f. (v.16)(Psalm 124; Isaiah 26:20-27) *"And the earth opened her mouth and swallowed up the flood..."* this is reminiscent of the delivery songs;

g. (Daniel 11:41; Matthew 24:16-21) The Jews are given access to a place of refuge;

In (13:7) a dual war is going on now. God is warring against the unbelieving world and Satan *(through the Beast)* is making war with the Saints.

(Matthew 24:22) the time is *shortened* for the sake of the elect or believing Jews.

Author's Point: Today, our job as "the elect" is to shorten the time of tribulation for the unsaved. How do we do this? Through evangelism, prayer and sharing the Word of God; we must "go into the highways and hedges and compel them to come" that their tribulation may be shortened. Someone prayed for you that you heeded the call to "come out of darkness into His marvelous light." Keep in mind ... *Someone shortened your "tribulation"*!

Practical lessons to be learned from this passage;

    a. Satan is at war with the Saints but our victory is in the Word of God

    b. Satan is the *accuser* of the brethren; how much "ammo" for accusation do you supply?

Presenter's Point: Satan is the accuser of the brethren; he is the father of lies; unfortunately, many of the accusations he makes against us are very true!

Author's Point: Though Satan is allowed to accuse the brethren, he cannot condemn;
(Romans 8:1) *"There is therefore now no condemnation to them which are in Christ Jesus, who walk not after the flesh but after the Spirit."*

    c. Beware! When we *accuse* the Saints, for we may be *unknowingly* joining forces with Satan; we must ever let love abide;

    d. Never be guilty of *opposing* the Jews ; it was through them that we received the savior;

Author's Point: We were grafted into the "olive tree" at the rejection of Christ by the Jews (John 1: 10 – 12). (Romans 11:23) God is able to restore Israel.

The Beast and the Anti-Christ (Romans 13)

This chapter introduces us to a dual calamity involving *"the two Beasts"*.

Author's Point: We must also understand that since John's book is a book of signs and symbols, the designation beasts does not necessarily mean animals. They are literally breathing, living, human beings, however, with animal like characteristics.
These verses present to us *The Satanic Trinity... Satan, the Beast and the false Prophet;*

1. The Anti-Christ; The Beast from the Sea (Revelation 13:1-10)

   a. (v. 1) *"... and he...)* This "he" is Satan, stands on the sands of the sea;*

   b. (Rev. 17: 15; 20:8) The sands of the *sea* represents the Gentile nations;

   c. (Rev. 17:10 – 12) explains the heads, horns and *crowns;*

      1. Seven heads: Seven mountains on which the harlot sits; seven kings, five have fallen; one is and the other is not come yet;

      2. Ten horns: Ten kings who have *not received a kingdom* as of yet; but receive authority for one hour with the Beast;

      3. **Read (Daniel 7) in its entirety very carefully.**

         • The Beasts represent four (4) separate and successive empires. Daniel saw:

         • The Lion: Babylon

         • The Bear: Medo-Persia

         • The Leopard: Greece

         • The "Little Horn" or fourth empire.

In (Daniel 7) Daniel records the same vision; however the order is reversed from that of John's vision. This is due to the vantage point of each prophet; John sees (1) the Little Horn (2) Leopard (3) Bear (4) Lion; the reverse order. Daniel looks *forward; John is looking back.*

Who is the Beast? Age old question! There are too many schools of thought to name them all. Many have tried to name him; add numbers to find his identity; and sought to identify him/her by other means.

Some have suggested Hitler; Stalin; Ronald (6) Wilson (6) Reagan (6) ...???

What we can surmise is:

- He will be *head of the Federation of European States working with the Roman Catholic Church;*

- He will cause Egypt and Russia to invade Palestine;

- Satan gives him power to do *great wonders;*

- He will cause people to receive and believe *the lie that he is 'god" and Christ is an imposter;*

- *He will cause the two witnesses to be slain during this time;*

- *He will ascend out of the abyss; the bottomless pit;*

- *He will be wounded fatally and completely recover;*

- *He is Satan's superman and will cause people to worship Satan;*

He that hath an Ear, Let Him Hear What the Spirit is saying to the Church

2. The False Prophet; The Beast from the Land (Revelation 13:11-18)

In chapters nineteen (19) and twenty (20) we are once again presented with what is called the *"Satanic Trinity"*;

a. Satan *counterfeits* the Father;

b. The Beast *counterfeits* the Son; the Savior;

c. The False Prophet *counterfeits* the Holy Spirit.

The second Beast comes from the *land, which we gather is Israel; Information points to the theory that he will be a Jew;*

a. *(Daniel 9:26b) determines that he will have Roman citizenship; the final "head" of the Roman Empire; but could be a Roman Jew;*

b. *The False Prophet assist in the ruling of the world;*

c. *He has horns (but no crowns, authority); the phrase **"like a lamb"** may suggest that he will begin ruling through peace and friendliness; his power, (same as the first beast) is given by Satan;*

d. *(Daniel 3) His task is to glorify the Beast*

e. *(Rev. 13:13; 11:5) he duplicates the miracles of the two witnesses just as (Exodus 7:11, 22, 8:7) Pharaoh's magicians duplicated the miracles of Aaron and Moses;*

f. *(2Thess. 2:9) This is consistent with Paul's prophecy of an Impersonating miracle worker; (Matthew 24:24) Christ Himself prophecies of this impersonator; so influential that if it were possible, "he would fool the very elect."*

g. **The False Prophet causes an image to be built of the Beast;**

   1. *The Image is alive and speaks great things and blasphemes against heaven*

2. *(Matthew 24:15; Daniel 11:45; 2Thess. 2:4) This is the "abomination of desolation!"*

(20:4) The False Prophet is not only interested in world religion but also worldwide economic control. He causes all to receive a mark in their forehead or in their hand which will allow him to control all buying and selling. Anyone not receiving the mark can neither buy nor sell. Those not receiving the mark will suffer greatly!

- Since Satan cannot touch Christ and the Saints in heaven, he will vent his hostility against the Saints on earth.

- The Mark...*666... the number of a man; (Irony) If you add up the first six numbers of the Roman Numeral system, the total 666 (I=1, v=5; x=10; l=50, c=100, d=500 totals 666) Could this reference a "revival of the Roman Empire"?*

- *(Daniel 3) Nebuchadnezzar's image is associated with the number (6); height threescore (60) cubits; breadth six (6) cubits;*

- *(1Samuel 17:4-7) Goliath associated with the number six (6); height six (6) cubits;*

   Six (6) is the number associated with man;
   Created on the sixth day;

   Given six (6) days to labor;

   Hours of his day based in six (4x6=24); Months of his year (2x6=12); minutes of his hour (6x10=60);

Author's Point: It is futile and non-profitable to try to juggle numbers to try to invent a man's name to associate with the Beast. *Only _trust Jesus now_ and make sure you're not here when "the Beast's" identity is revealed!*

Revelation Chapter 14

The Voice of the *144,000* (Revelation 14:1-5)

This *special group of men were sealed by God before the seventh seal was opened (Revelation 7). Now they are seen on Mount Zion with the Lord Jesus Christ. This picture is in direct contrast with the one depicted in (Revelation 13); those are the followers of the Beast whose mark is in their forehead; God will always retain a remnant for Himself.*

*The 144,000 are **standing** with Christ on Mount Zion. Theological schools of thought differ as to whether this is a heavenly scene or earthly scene. Since events are **raptured** in chapter 4 and the scene seems to anticipate Christ's coronation and the establishment of the kingdom when He returns to earth (second coming), this author leans toward this being a heavenly scene.*

Some say that since John hears the voice "from" heaven, it is likely or may suggest that the scene is taking place on earth. More food for this train of thought is that Christ is enthroned in the heavenly Zion (Psalm 2:6) and we are also with Him (Ephesians 2:6).

Either way, the scene anticipates the coming kingdom on earth; we see that the "four beast" or living creatures will also be there.

The 144,000 are not only *standing but;*

1. *(v.2,3) they are singing; (Pss.33:3; 40:3; 96:1) a new song;*

All sorrows are turned into songs.

2. *(Revelation 14:4,5) these are separated, (sanctified); do not belong to the earth (not earth minded) but are redeemed out of the earth;*

3. *(Philippians 3:17-21; John 17:14-19) We are not to be partakers of the world system; we are not our own but bought with a price.*

4. *(v.8) they are not defiled with women; this is spiritual defilement; (James 4:4) not a physical defilement; these were faithful to God and did not receive the mark of the Beast.*

5. *(Leviticus 23:9-14) they were a type of "first fruits"; the very best; the finest of the harvest that is soon to follow.*

The Pouring out of the Vials (Revelation 14:6-13)

Three Angelic messengers are now brought on the scene. Each one has a ***special announcement:***

1. **The Everlasting Gospel (vv. 6-7)** *"And I saw another angel ... "* in today's times, God uses men to give His message. It is a message of salvation, repentance and deliverance. However, in these last days; in this period of judgment, angels are used. The message is *not* concerned with the *Savior* but rather the *Creator and warns of impending, eminent* judgment. The *message* is meant to cause men to fear and reverence God and be saved.

2. **The fall of Babylon (v. 8)** *"...and there followed another angel saying Babylon is fallen..."* though this event is alluded to here, the actual event will take place in chapters seventeen (17) and eighteen (18). *Babylon* is in reference to the apostate *religious-system* headed up by the Beast in conjunction with Rome.
(Further scriptural references; (Jeremiah 50:14, 15, 38 and 51:7-8).

3. **The Final Judgment (v. 9-13)** In **(Revelation 15-18)** we have the seven vials judgment. It is said to be *poured out without mixture;* there will be no *grace and no mercy mingled with this wrath.* All who wear the *mark of the Beast* will be tormented without rest or relief.

   In contrast, at this time, the Saints will be at rest from their labors and be blessed. Which would you rather; **rest or wrath?**

The choice is yours (Joshua 24:15). Certainly (14:13) *"Blessed are the dead that die in the Lord"* refers to Tribulation Saints but can also be applied to NOW!

4. **The Fighting of the Battle of Armageddon (14:14-20)** In this portion of scripture, John sees Christ coming on a cloud with a sickle in hand.

    In contrast to the first advent, He came as a rejected sewer (Matthew 13: 3-23); He comes now in judgment to reap the harvest.

    The Second angels declares; *"the harvest is ripe!"* Nothing is judged *before its time!*

Review of events leading up to the Battle of Armageddon:

During the first half of the Tribulation, while the Beast is working in association with the Jews, Russia and Egypt will attack Israel. The Beast will be forced to go to Palestine in keeping with his covenant with the Jews. God defeats Russia; the Beast defeats Egypt. At this time the Beast sets himself up as the world ruler, reigning from Jerusalem. After Babylon is destroyed, the enemies of the Beast have their opportunity to attack. Armies will advance towards Palestine during the last half of the tribulation to fight against the Beast.

Dr. Pentecost suggests that the Battle will be more of a campaign than just a battle. It seems to rest more in a series of battles coming to a head in the great battle at Megiddo. According to (Revelation 19:17-21), the forces will array against each other until Christ comes back "with the Church"; the armies will then join forces seeking to defeat Christ. Of course, Christ defeats the armies with the "Sword of His mouth". This marks the beginning of the Millennium!

(Isaiah 66:1-6) and (Joel 3) give further material on this final battle;

Taken from Dr. Warren W. Wiersby.

We have here a simile of a man cutting grapes from a vine. The world system is the "vine of the earth" while Jesus is the only *"True Vine"* (John 15). Israel was planted in the world to bring forth good fruit and to be God's holy vine. Instead she rejected the "husbandman" and went after the false christ. Now Israel must suffer the consequences of her very costly mistake. It costs way too much to go to hell. Don't pay the fare!!!

The Fighting of the Battle of Armageddon

(V. 20) represent a terrible picture of judgment and bloodshed. Alford seems to think that there are two groups of "grapes to the vine"; one being Saints (v. 14) and the other (vv. 15, 16) sinners. I am of the persuasion that they both are wicked. Two GREEK words are used for "ripe". However, they both refer to the condition of the grapes for judgment; the first (v. 14) {GREEK, EXERANTHE} gives the indication of *overripe or rotten; in verse (v. 18)* fully ripe {GREEK, EKMASAN} references *fully grown or in prime condition. This meaning does not necessarily promote good grapes; rather having received all opportunities for repentance, they are fully ripe for judgment. (v.19) tells us they are gathered and cast into the winepress of God's wrath.*

The blood is said to run (180-200) miles out of the city. (v.20) gives us an awful picture of blood running as **"high as the horses bridle."** *Whether this is a literal or figurative assessment really doesn't make much difference. It is an awful, awful day and it is surely to come!*

William Kelly regards this chapter as an outline of major events at the end of the Age: (1) the appearance of the godly remnant of Israel; (2) a testimony to Gentiles; (3) the fall of Babylon; (4) the doom of the worshipers of the beast; (5) the blessedness of saints who are martyred; (6) the harvest; (7) the wrath of God on the world (*Lectures on the Book of Revelation*, p. 330).

Beatitude: (Rev. 14:13) Blessed are the dead which die in the Lord from henceforth; yea, for they may rest from their labor and their works do follow them.

Seven Vials of Wrath
Chapter 15

The Seven Bowls Judgment

A Glorious Heavenly Scene; Here John gazes upon two (2) scenes:

1. **The Victors and their Song** (Revelation 15:1-4)
    a. (Revelation 12:11; 13:7-10) These are believed to be the Tribulation Saints who refused to bow to the Beast; these are they which lost their lives for the sake of Christ;
    b. John sees them *standing, in victory, by the heavenly sea;* everyone that loses his life for Christ's sake will find everlasting life;
    c. The *Sea of Glass* here is *mingled with fire; back in* (4:6), the *sea* was clear; the presence of *fire* denotes the wrath of God and His judgment;
    d. (v.3) They sing the *song of Moses*,(Exodus 15; Psalm 118:14; Isaiah 21:1) and the song of the Lamb;*

*The Lord is my strength and song; and He is become my salvation"!

Author's Point: We see here the unifying of *the law* and *grace; Moses and the Lamb;* God's law is being vindicated and Grace is at work!

2. **The Vials and Their Significance** (Revelation 15:5-8)

    a. (v.1) The angels carry the bowls of *the last plagues; (Revelation 10:7) Christ announced that the* mystery of God's *wrath is filled up or completed;* there will be *no more delay;*

    b. (v. 5) Since the Beast has desecrated the earthly temple, the Heavenly temple is now opened; God will keep His covenant with Israel; *Many believers will flee to (Edom, Moab and Ammon) where God will protect them; many others will be slain for their testimony;*

    c. Seven angels *(completion; perfection)* come out of the temple;

    d. They come out of the *Holy of Holies;*

    e. (Revelation 1:13) Their garments, *pure and white linen; golden girdles,* signify **holiness;**

The Vials and their Significance

The heavenly temple is now filled with *smoke* from the glory of God:

a. (Exodus 40:34, 35) When the OT tabernacle was dedicated, God's glory filled the tent;

b. (II Chronicles 7:1-4) when the OT temple was dedicated, God's glory again filled the temple;

The difference here is that there is smoke mingled with the glory. This is a sign of *judgment!*

Students of prophecy are not in total agreement as to the arrangement of these judgment; seals, trumpets and vials. Some believe that these judgments follow in succession, or after each other, i.e., *the seventh seals lead to the trumpets; the seventh trumpet leads to the vials. If this is true, it seems that* the trumpets and vials are <u>contained in the seals!</u> *This might be suggestive of the seals being opened throughout the tribulation.*

Some theologians hold that the first *six* seals cover the first three and a half years and that the seventh seal, inclusive of the trumpets and vials, cover the last three and a half years.

Norman Harrison puts the *seals and trumpets in the first three and a half years; the vials in the last half.*

Author's Point: God has not given us all information in plain order and precise details. As stated earlier; some signs are revealed and many others are not. Some others will become clearer as time progresses. However, all that we need in order to be *escaped* from this turmoil has been given to us; "*receive the Lord Jesus as your Savior and Lord; confess Him with your mouth and believe in your heart that God has raised Him from the dead and YOU <u>SHALL BE SAVED</u> from this hour!*

The Seven Vials of the Wrath of God (Revelation 16)

Comparing your notes of Revelation 8, we see the parallel between the trumpet judgments and the vial judgments. In each case, the judgment affects the same things (the same areas), but the vial judgments are more severe. It seems too that the vial judgments occur in quick succession, aimed especially at the Beast and his satanic kingdom. These afflictions prepare the way for **Armageddon** *and* **the return of Christ to earth** *to claim His kingdom.*

1. **(Revelation 16:1, 2) (first angel) GRIEVOUS SORES;**

    a. (Exodus 9:9) this is reminiscent of the *sixth* plagues of Egypt; *the word noisome has as its root "to annoy"; to be troublesome or vexing;*

    b. (Deuteronomy 28:27) God promised this plague upon Israel if they rebelled against him;

    c. In (v. 11) the sores are still present when the *fifth* vial is poured out; the afflictions do not soften their *hard* hearts; men still curse and blaspheme God.

2. **(Revelation 16:3-7) (second and third angel) WATERS TURNED TO BLOOD;**

    a. (Exodus 7:17, 18; Psalm 105:29) reminiscent of the *first* plague of Egypt; (v. 3) the sea turned to blood; also (chapter 8:8) the trumpets;

In the trumpet judgment, only a *part* of the sea is affected; here the entire water system is affected.

The angels of the waters *praise* God for His actions and explain that these judgments are fair; i.e., (Exodus) Pharaoh drowned the Jewish boys; his armies were drowned in the Red Sea; (Esther) Haman built a gallows to hang Mardecai and he was hanged on it himself. The Hymnologist has penned "dig one ditch, you better dig two"…, however, Saints know that, in God, It only takes *one ditch!* *"Vengeance is mine, sayeth the Lord."*

The Seven Vials of the Wrath of God

3. **(Revelation 16:8-11) (fourth and fifth angels) SCORCHING SUN AND DARKNESS.** *The judgments from the fourth and fifth angels involve the heavens.*

   a. (v. 8) the *fourth angel* pours out his vial and causes the sun to scorch men. Note the power is given to the *angel,* not the sun;

   b. (v. 9) (Daniel 5:22) men were scorched with great heat from the sun *but repented not;*

   c. (Malachi 4:1-2) The prophet promised this day would *"burn as an oven";*

   d. (v. 10) (Exodus 10:21-23) is synonymous with the *ninth plague of Egypt)* The *fifth angel* reverses the scene and pours out *darkness* on the seat of the Beast;

It is possible that this darkness is not universal but only covers the immediate kingdom of the Beast, where *his seat is.*

Satan is called the *prince of darkness.* It seems but poetic justice that darkness should invade his kingdom.

   e. (Joel 2:1, 2) the seer prophesied that the Day of the Lord would be a day of darkness; (Mark 13:24) Christ declares "in those days...the sun shall be darkened, and the moon shall not give her light";

Can you imagine the agony of the scorching boils that will not heal and having to endure this trauma in utter darkness? Thank God for a *means of escape.*

William Newell: *Men who will not be won by grace will not be won at all.*

Accept Christ or prepare to *face the heat!*

The Gathering of the Armies (Revelation 16:12-16)

When God delivered Israel from the bondage of Egypt, He dried up the Red Sea to secure their exit. Here in Revelation, He dries up part of the great river Euphrates to allow the armies of the kings of the east to meet the armies of the nations of the world at Armageddon.

    a. (v. 14) the word *"battle"* used here would be better rendered *"campaign"* as it is more a series of wars consummating in the great Battle of Armageddon.

Historical Point: Russia and her allies invade Palestine about the *middle* of the tribulation period (Gog and Magog, *Ezekiel 38, 39)* and are judged by the Lord. With this, the Beast seized complete control of the *world system.* Russia, the kings of the east and Egypt now join forces to battle against the Beast and his armies at Armageddon, AKA; mountain *of Megiddo.*

    a. (vv. 13, 14) The *Satanic trinity* uses demons like frogs *(figurative)* to assemble these armies. Three (3) demons are used; (1) out of the mouth of the dragon, (2) out of the mouth of the Beast and (3) out of the mouth of the False Prophet;

    b. (Matthew 14:29-30) these armies will assemble to fight against the Lord. *They first assemble to fight Jerusalem then combine their forces to fight the Lord at His return with His bride, the church.*

    c. Read also (Joel 3:9-14; Zephaniah 3:8; Zechariah 12, Isaiah 24:1-8).

    d. (v. 15) assures the Saints that they will not be caught *"in the dark"*; (Matthew 24:43) *watchfull-ness* is encouraged;

    e. (Revelation 18:4) Christ commands the Saints to *keep themselves out of the world system;* Keep free of the defilement of the satanic system; In other words, *keep your garments clean!*

The Mystery of God, Finished (Revelation 16: 17-21)

In (10:6, 7) God promised that the *Mystery of God* would be finished after the seventh angel poured out his vial; now we see this prophecy and promise fulfilled.

The events described in this section look forward to the fall of Babylon (v. 19) and the final return of Christ (*second coming*)to reign for a thousand years *(millennium). Chapters 17 and 18 are included in the seventh vial judgment.*

 a. (v. 17) the seventh angel pours out his vial *into the air;* (Ephesians 2:2) Satan is referred to as *the prince of the powers of the air;* the *Master's* judgment is directed at the *master-mind behind the corruption, Satan himself!*

From this point on, Christ will deal with (Rev. 17) Satan's religious system, (Rev. 18) his political system, his armies and in (chapter 20), Satan himself;

 b. (v. 19) Dr. W. W. Wiersby seems to think that the term *great city* refers to Jerusalem, being divided into three (3) parts; **However this author is of the persuasion that this is in reference to the great city Babylon.**

 c. (v. 21) hail out of heaven, reminiscent of the seventh plague of Moses (Exodus 9:22-26); every *stone* about the weight of a *talent:* about 125 pounds.

With all this judgment, men continue to blaspheme. (Leviticus 24:16) states that blasphemers should be *stoned to death; therefore the hail stones is but a fitting judgment.*

(v. 17) IT IS DONE!!! The hymnologist declares; *Hallelujah, 'tis done; I believe in God's Son; I am saved by the blood of the crucified One!!! Praise God!!! It is done. This is also reminiscent of the cry of Our Lord from the cross of Calvary..."IT IS FINISHED"!!!*

The Harlot and Her Daughters (Desolation and Destruction) (Revelation 17)

Babylon, the source of many heathen and pagan religions which have all opposed the faith of Israel and the faith of the church...is here seen in its final judgment. These chapters do not necessarily fall in chronological order as with the seals, trumpets and bowls of the wrath of God, and many theologians find it difficult to determine the precise meaning of what is being revealed in these chapters.

Beginning in chapter 17, John describes the Lamb's "step-by-step" victory over the Beast and his kingdom. As related earlier, in (17) the religious system is judged; in (18), the political and economic system are judged. Finally, the Lord Himself returns to earth (second coming), Judges Satan, the Beast, and the false prophet and proceeds to establish His own Kingdom.

*John continues to use symbolisms to relate his points: (Rev. 19:7, 8) the church of Christ is a pure virgin; whereas the false religious system, Babylon, is called a **harlot: she has abandoned the truth and prostituted herself for personal gain;***

Unfortunately, every generation continues to have its "dose" of a "Babylon"; a political and economic system that has sought to capture the minds and destinies of people. God is still, as always, calling us to "come out from among them and be Holy, (virgin) even as He is Holy!

The Invitation (Revelation 17:1, 2) One of the seven angels who brought about the climax of God's wrath invites John to "come and see the judgment of the great whore that sat upon *many waters; the final world system;*

Four "women" are mentioned in the Book of Revelation;

   a. (2:20) *Jezebel, apostasy creeping in to the church through false teachings;*

   b. (12:1) *Israel;*

   c. (Chapter 17) *the harlot, final apostate world system;*

   d. (19:7) *the Bride, the Church.*

The Explanation (Revelation 17:3-18) there are several *symbols* used in this portion of the text.

(v. 7) Thankfully, God has provided an explanation to us through the angel that summonses John!

a. (v. 3) <u>The Woman</u>; *sat on a scarlet colored beast;* full of names of blasphemy; having seven heads and ten horns; in (v. 18) *the angel explains that she is a* **city; the great city, that reigns over the kings of the earth;**

b. <u>The City</u> *(v. 3) the seven heads are identified as seven mountains in (v.9); situated on seven hills, (1) Aventine (2) Caelian (3) Capitoline (4) Esquiline (5) Palatine (6) Quirinal and (7) Viminal; this is the city of Rome;*

c. (v. 3) <u>*Scarlet colored* Beast</u>, *(links him with the Dragon); this is the same Beast as in (chapter 13), the anti-christ; (v.8) was, and is not, and yet is; shall ascend out of the bottomless pit and go into perdition;*

1. (John 17:12) the designation perdition links the Beast with Judas who "went down into perdition";

d. *(v.10) states that the seven heads are seven kings; five are fallen, one is and the other is yet to come! Following are suggestive placements based upon history:*

Five Fallen Kingdoms: Egypt, Assyria, Babylon, Persia and Greece;
Fallen Rulers: Julius Caesar, Tiberius, Caligula, Claudius, and Nero

One that is: Rome; Domitian, in John's day;

One to come: the Beast, of the revived Roman Empire

e. *(v. 11) the beast that was and is not, is the eighth, and is of the seven and goes into perdition; this is to say that one of the seven will "rise" again for a return reign;*

f. *(v.12) the ten horns (Daniel 7:20)* **are ten kings that have not received a kingdom but will receive "power" for one (the) hour with the Beast;**

The Explanation

The *ten horns* are synonymous with the ten *toes* of the image (Daniel 7:20) of Daniel's vision. The *woman* commits fornications with the kings of the earth and for a while dominates them.

> h. (v. 13, 17) *the kings of the earth now have one mind and give their authority to this great enemy of God;*
>
> > 1. (Romans 8:7) *the carnal mind (the minding of the flesh) is enmity against God; the Beast goes out to make war against the Lamb;*
>
> i. (v. 16) it is important to note here that the *kings of the earth* turn on the whore **"and shall make her desolate and naked" and shall destroy her.**

(v.17) assures us that God is still in control of all actions. The coming together of the minds of the enemy is at God's command *"until the words of God be fulfilled".*

> j. (v.15) the waters; where the *whore sits* are nations, and tongues, and peoples. These are the people of the earth and the whore shall have influence over the whole world; *politically, economically and religiously;*

The Application

The whore **represents the apostate church still to be manifested and centered in Rome. The name Babylon is associated with the whore also. It takes us back to (Genesis 10) where the first organized rebellion against God was initiated; the tower of Babel. This represented *confusion* and gives itself to all apostate religions.**

This is not just Roman rebellion but carries with it every so-called religion and anti-Christian system that has killed God's people for centuries. It appears that many groups will move closer to the Roman way and will form one great world church. The *church will become powerful with the help of the Beast. This world church (whore)* will ride into power on the *back* of the Beast, Satan and the *Federated States of Europe. This will give Rome its greatest power.*

(Revelation 6:1, 2) Remember, the first seal, the white horse?

The Beast will get the support of the *ten kings of the earth* so that there will be a union between the nations of Europe, the Beast and the world church; As revealed in scripture chronology, the events of (chapter 17) actually take place in the first half of the tribulation for the Beast has not yet been revealed in his *true satanic character.*

(Chapter 13) Now, here the Beast will want to exercise sole authority. Therefore, at the mid-point of the tribulation ... *the whore* will have to go! *The whore, the apostate church,* represents the *"worship of God."* The Beast cannot have this or any resemblance of God worship, even if it is *apostate.*

So, we see (v.16), the Federated Nations of Europe will turn against the *world church* and destroy it. (Revelation 2:20-23) is hereby fulfilled. At this time, the Beast will set himself up as "god" and demand worship for himself from the nations.

We can see tidbits of this world church forming today. The New York Times carries a column today (9/22/2009) of a coming visit (October 20) of the Pope to New York to address the United Nations on its fiftieth anniversary. In 1979, during the second Vatican Council, Pope Paul VI visited the U.N.; a visit which brought profound changes to the church.

Last August, the Pope spent four (4) days in the U.S. where he addressed over 400,000 young Catholics gathered for a *World Youth Day.* (N.Y. Times, 9-22-09).

Could these be steps toward a World Church?

The Apostate Church is called The Whore; the True Church of the Lamb is referred to as "*the* virgin bride";

The Apostate Church is In the wilderness; whereas the Church of Christ is in heaven;

The Apostate Church is adorned by Satan; the Church of Christ is adorned by Christ;

The Apostate church is judged forever; the Church of Christ reigns forever;

The Apostate church is stained with the blood of the martyrs; the Church of Christ is redeemed by the blood of the Lamb;

*As the **called out ones**, we must sanctify ourselves from Satan's false church **(come out from among them)** and be true to Christ and the Word of God. The world church only appears to be successful but as all of Satan's promises, they are empty, seasonal and temporary.*

Our hope is built on nothing less than Jesus' blood and righteousness. Built on things eternal!!!

NOTE: We can see many signs today that suggest that the governments of our world Is becoming more and more global; financial systems are essentially global; commerce, with the introduction of the internet and expanding free trade is global; there is a convergence in the world's political governance such as the European Economic Community and the increasing power and jurisdiction of the United Nations.

We are continually seeing signs of spiritual idolatry in our world and in the churches. The "New Age" movement that encourages "spiritualism" that teaches that we are our own "gods"; the churches that leave Christ out of the equation saying to their congregations that living a so-called good life is all that's needed to get to heaven. There are movements that teach a compromising gospel and a tolerance for immoral behavior and same sex marriages. Without a doubt, these are the last days and the world is set for the appointed time.

The Harlot and Her Daughters (Desolation and Destruction) (Revelation 18)

In this chapter, we have commercial, economic Babylon which represents the great *worldwide* system of the latter days. The apostate church will have a part also in the economics of the nations. When the religious system collapses, it will be the beginning of the end for the whole system of the Beast, even though he will have another 3&1/2 half years (*"the final hour")* to reign. Keep in mind that this is all included in the *fulfilling of the Word of God.*

In this chapter are four different voices:

1. The Voice of Judgment (Revelation 18:1-3)

The announcement of *fallen Babylon* was also made in (14:8) and (16:9). This angels announcement and the repetition of *"is fallen, is fallen"* may be suggest of the *dual judgment; religious* Babylon and *economic* Babylon.

> a. (v.6) states that Babylon would receive *double* for her sins;
>
> b. (Ephesians 2:22) *the church should be,"...built together for a habitation of God through the Spirit." However,*
>
> c. (v.2) she has become a habitation for devils, every foul spirit, and a cage for every unclean and hateful bird; *(Matthew 13:4; 19) Satan is pictured as a bird (evil one);*
>
> d. (v.3) her influence over the nations of the earth has been as though *men were drunk with much wine.* She has made them rich and this seems to be all that matters to them.

2. The Voice of Separation (Revelation 18:4-8)

At this point, John hears another voice from heaven calling for *sanctification.* Some of the people of God are in the city and God wants them to *come out of her* for at least two (2) reasons;

The Voice of Separation (Revelation 18:4-8) the reasons being:

1. The city will be destroyed;

2. The city is *satanic* and God does not want His people defiled;

(2Corinthians 6:14-17) "Come out" has ever been the call to the people of God for <u>salvation</u> means <u>separation,</u> (*sanctification*) from the world and its ways. John shares with us in his 1st Epistle that we should *"love not the world neither the things that are in the world. If a man loves the world, the love of the father is not in him."*

> **a.** (v.7) the world glorifies itself; the Christian seeks to glorify God; notice the bragging of this *"Babylon", **"I sit a queen...and shall see no sorrow"**;*

> b. (v.8) **"in one day...** her joys will be turned into sorrows." All who have been partakers of her joy will drink of her sorrows.

> (1Timothy 5:22) "...neither be partakers of other men's sins."

3. The Voice of Mourning (Revelation 18:8-19)

We see here two (2) groups lamenting the fall of Babylon;

1. (vv. 9, 10) the kings of the earth;

2. (vv. 11-19) the merchants of the earth; as they behold the "smoke of her burning; (Jeremiah 50:46).

Author's Point: These have committed *fornications with Babylon and rejected the True and Living God; loving and going after idols, predominantly, riches, money; (1Timothy 6:10) "the love of money." They danced to her music, now the Piper must be paid! The lap of luxury has come to an end.*

> 3. (vv. 10, 16, 19) the use of *"alas, alas..." gives us an indication of double recompense for her sins: destruction was total in just "one hour".*

The Voice of Mourning

Why do the merchants and kings lament the demise of the *"great whore"?*

1. (v.12, 13) their *merchandiser* is now gone; including the great wealth of the merchant system and also *"slaves and souls of men."*

2. (Acts 16:19) *this same scenario is played out when Paul was at Philippi. A certain damsel brought much profit to her masters through soothsaying. Paul cast the demon out of her and when the masters saw that their source of gain was gone, they brought Paul and Silas before the magistrates.*

There will be an all out increase in slavery in these last days. Satan has always sought to enslave the hearts and minds of mankind; (2Peter 2:3) to mislead and lead men away from the teachings and directives of God.

**Many believe that this *great whore church* is a form of *apostate Christendom; a world religion that has betrayed Christianity and is interlocked with the pagan, godless governments of the world.* (G.H. Pember; *The antichrist, Babylon and the Coming of the Kingdom, 1886).*

4.The Voice of Rejoicing (Revelation 18:20-24)

We find here in this passage as in (Isaiah 55:8, 9), mankind of the earth still has not the same viewpoint as God. When Satan was cast out of heaven, heaven rejoiced but the earth mourned; here now, Babylon is destroyed; heaven rejoices and the earth laments. Why does heaven rejoice?

a. (Revelation 6:9-11) The martyrs asked the question ... "how long, Oh Lord...? (Romans 12:19) The blood of the martyrs has now been avenged and the question answered.

b. (Revelation 18:21) the casting of the millstone indicates the suddenness of God's judgment against the Beast;

(Jeremiah 25:9-11; Jeremiah 51) In this chapter, we are admonished here to take note of the repeated use of the phrase *"no more"* ; *the judgment has been levied and there is nothing that can be done to alter it. All that remains is for Christ to destroy the armies of the Beast! We are in the era of No More!*

1. (v.22) the voice of harpers and musicians and pipers shall be heard *"no more…"; no more craftsman of any craft; the sound of a millstone shall be heard "no more";*

2. (v.23) *the light of a candle shall shine "no more"; the voice of the bridegroom (Christ) and of the bride (Church) shall be heard "no more";*

What will be seen and heard in her;

1. (v.24) The blood of prophets and of saints and of all that were slain upon the earth;

With the marriage of leopard beast and lamb beast, Babylon, the adultery of church and world is doomed. As it goes down, all heaven will resound with the *"highest praise"; Hallelujah*! After this follows the refrain of the wedding procession as the Lamb espouses to Himself His true bride, the virgin church!!!*Praise be to God!!!*

Author's Point: With the present condition of the church; its imperfections and short comings; one may wonder, (Sermon) *"How in the world are we going to get the church ready for the Lord?" The fact is, It is not our duty to get it ready (praise God for that). (Ephesians 5: 25b-27) The scripture is emphatic in that it assures us that Christ will present the church to Himself a glorious church, not having spot or wrinkle, or any such thing!!! Thank God! The true church will be ready!!!*

My God's gettin' us ready for that Great Day!!!

The Two Suppers (Revelation 19)

The Destruction of the Beast and the False Prophet

These verses present the climax of the wrath of God as Jesus Christ comes to destroy the armies of the nations of the world. Shouts of *hallelujah* fill the air as John hears the roar of a great multitude in heaven shouting and lifting up their God in glory and praises.

Hallelujah is used nowhere else in the New Testament; however, it is employed *four times* in the first six (6) verses of chapter nineteen.

Author's Point: *Shouting, singing, praises, joyful noises;* where will there be room for the *quiet saints?* I often wonder of this when I see supposedly saved and sanctified saints who are so quiet in worship. Our worship experiences today are to be a *dress rehearsal* for kingdom living. It is difficult for me to imagine God requiring of us *joyful noise* and then endowing us with a *quiet spirit.*

1. **The Anthems of Joy in Heaven (Revelation 19:1-10)**

    There are four "hallelujah choruses" here as all of heaven anticipates the return of Christ to the earth.

Author's Point: The promise of the return of Christ to the earth should cause us all to live constantly in a state of *expectation and anticipation.* Living thusly is as Christ as prescribed... (Matthew 24:24)"be ye also ready for you know not the moment or the hour the Son of Man shall come". Getting ready is not good enough for you can still be left, getting ready!

Beatitude: Blessed are they which are called to the marriage supper of the Lamb.
Why does heaven rejoice?

   a. (v.1, 2) because the sin of the great harlot has been judged and completed; (v.1,3,4) This completion of judgment merits and receives, *three (3)* hallelujahs;

The Anthems of Joy in Heaven

Author's Point: Note here how the four and twenty elders *fall down and worship* God that sat on the throne. What a lesson to us as saints of God! We should never be too high minded to fall prostrate before the God of the universe. Humility and humbleness are trademarks of true worship. *Hallelujah! He is worthy!*

> b. (vv.5, 6) because God is reigning; He is on the throne and *HE IS GOD! Omnipotent...He reigns with all Power;*

> c. (vv.7-10) (2Corinthians 11:2) because the marriage of the Lamb is come; (has been completed); *that I (He) may present you as a chaste virgin to Christ;*

(v.7) the bride has "...*made herself ready*"; in this we find that the church will be judged on "deeds". This is to say, in a manner of speaking, each of us will wear the garments of our own making for the deeds of our life will "make up the wedding gown." How will you be dressed? Your attire will reflect your faithfulness and vice-versa.

We, as saints of the Church Age *(Pentecost to Rapture)* are not invited to the wedding supper for we are the *guest of honor, the Bride of Christ.* However, the OT Saints and rejuvenated Israel will be invited to share in the glory.

> 2. **The Armies of Jesus Christ From Heaven ((Revelation 19:11-16)**
>
> In (Rev. 4:1) the Church is raptured and heaven opens to let her in; here heavens opens to let Christ and His armies ride forth in victory; (Matthew 25:31) This army is made up of **OT** Saints, the church and the angels; In Revelation 6:1, the *false, impersonating christ rode a white horse; BUT here the* Faithful and True (Rev. 1:5, 3:7, 14) *rides forth to judge and make war.*

The Armies of Jesus Christ from Heaven

Beatitude: Blessed are they which are called unto the marriage supper of the Lamb.

The description of Christ;

    a. (v.11) He rides a *fiery* white horse;

    b. (v.12) His eyes are as *flames of fire; all things shall be tried by fire; on His head are many crowns; He had a name written that no man knew except Himself;*

    c. (v.13) He was clothed with a vesture dipped in blood; HIS NAME IS CALLED "THE WORD OF GOD"; (John 1:1)

Judgment and righteousness go hand in hand. *His judgments are righteous. He is the Righteous Judge.*

    d. (V.15) *"Out of His mouth went a sharp sword";*

    e. (v.16) He has on His vesture and on His thigh a name written, (Psalm 72) KING OF KINGS and LORD OF LORDS; this is *indisputable pre-eminence.*

He comes now to *rule with a rod of iron; He comes to tread the winepress of the wrath of God at the Battle of Armageddon. He is Conquering King of kings!*

The armies of the world have gathered *together* in Palestine to fight against the Beast and his armies. However, when they see the *sign of the coming of the Lord,* they will unite to oppose Him.

NOTE: Have you notice that enemies will unite to oppose an *outsider. Police officers say that domestic disputes are among the most dangerous calls they must answer for many times the abused party will join forces with the abuser to oppose the officers.*

3. The Announcement of Judgment on Earth (Revelation 19:17-21)

Two (2) suppers are mentioned in this portion of the text; (v.9) the marriage supper of the Lamb; and (v.17) the supper of the great God; this is Armageddon! One is a festive and happy occasion; the other is a time of judgment and sorrow;

   a. (vv.17, 18) *"...that you may eat the flesh of..."* the angel, *standing in the sun,* announces the *complete destruction* on all opposing forces; note the list of the destroyed; **captains, mighty men, horses and their riders;** none are a match for God.

   b. (v.18) *flesh; flesh; flesh; flesh;* flesh is no match for God and is enmity against God; flesh can never please God; flesh does not change. God has condemned flesh; (Genesis 6:12) *for all flesh has corrupted his way.*

(v.19) *"... the beast, and the kings of the earth ... "* Who are these armies come *to-gather* against Christ? These are the armies of the *Ten Kingdom* Federation of Europe, the kings of the East, Egypt, and Russia. They gather on the *Plains of Esdraelon* in Palestine; called by Napoleon the most *"natural battle field in the world."* **This is the Mount of Megiddo; this is Armageddon!**

(v.20) *"...he deceived them that received the mark ... '* The followers of the Beast are "marked" men. The mark of the Beast on their bodies (forehead or hand) set them for certain death. Not only does Christ destroy the armies of the Beast but the Beast and the False Prophet are captured and "cast alive into a lake of fire burning with brimstone."*

Men who would not receive the Gospel and salvation *through the Word* will ultimately be slain *by the Word.*

The Prophets Isaiah (63), Zachariah (14) and Joel (2-3) have much to say concerning this great battle. Who can prevail against God?

Ride on, King Jesus, Ride on; No man can hinder Thee!

THE MILLENNIUM; THE LAST JUDGMENT; THE NEW JERUSALEM AND ETERNITY. REVELATION 20:1-22:50)

The Great White Throne Judgment (Revelation 20)

This is the *"thousand years"* chapter that deals with the doctrine of *the millennium.* The word has as its meaning in Latin, "THOUSAND YEARS". Some deny that there will be a literal thousand-year reign of Christ on earth.

However, this author believes that, "according to the scriptures" there will be this literal thousand year kingdom for several reasons:

    a. (Luke 1:30-33) *it fulfills the* **OT** *prophecy to Israel;*

    b. *it gives a* public display *of Christ's glory to the nations of Israel;*

    c. It answers the prayer of *"thy kingdom come";*

    d. It fulfills the promises to the church that the saints will reign with Christ;

    e. (Romans 8:19-22) Its brings about the complete redemption of nature as promised;

    f. It gives man one final trial under the sovereign rule of Christ.

1. **Before the Millennium (Revelation 20:1-5).**

   The Battle of Armageddon is over!; the Beast and False Prophet have been cast into the Lake of Fire; now Christ lays hold on *that Old Serpent, Satan* and cast him into the Bottomless Pit.

       a. (2Peter 2:4; Jude 6) shows us that some of Satan's followers have all ready been chained;

       b. (Revelation 17:8) the Beast came out of the bottomless pit and was cast into hell; his final judgment is not yet come;

Before the Millennium

After Satan is cast down, then takes place the resurrection of the tribulation saints who gave their lives in faithful service to Christ.

> a. (Daniel 12:1-3) *it appears that, according to Daniel's prophecy, the OT saints will rise at this time;*

These cannot be raised at the time of the Rapture for this is the *time of the Church Age saints.* At this time also, there are no more saints in the realm of the dead (Hades). They have been resurrected to reign with Christ. This is known as the *First Resurrection, which begins with the rapture of the church.*

The hymnologist refrains: *"Where shall I be when the first trumpet sound? Where shall I be when it sounds so loud? It sounds so loud that it wakes up the dead. Oh, where shall I be when it sounds?"*

The first resurrection includes the rapture of the church (1Thessalonians 4:13) up to the resurrection of the tribulation saints (Rev. 20:4); All these are saved and will not have a part in the *second death, or eternal separation from God.*

Author's Point: Dr. Wiersby states that the OT saints knew of the "resurrection of the dead" but were not aware of a *"called out"* resurrection from *among* the dead, as was Jesus raised from among the dead. This is taught in (Mk. 9:9, 10). There is no record of a "general" resurrection in the bible. The saved are raised at different times in the first resurrection. The lost are raised in the *second resurrection.* There is a time span of one-thousand years (millennium) between the two resurrections.

> a. (v.1,2) an Angel comes down with the key of the bottomless pit and lays hold on Satan and bounds him for a thousand years;

> b. (v.4) Thrones are prepared for the purified nation of Israel, the Church and the tribulation saints to reign with Christ.

c. (Matthew 25:31-46) gives us a picture of Gentiles being judged (separated) prior to the Millennium as *sheep on the right and goats on the left.* Believers will *"enter into the joy of the Kingdom"; everlasting life!*

The Great White Throne Judgment

2. During the Millennium (Revelation 20:6)

The millennial kingdom will be Christ's *divine rule* upon earth. No sin or injustice will be permitted. Christ will rule with a *rod of iron.*

a. (Isaiah 2:1-4) Jerusalem will be the center of the kingdom.

b. (Matthew 19:28) the disciples will reign with Christ;

c. (Isaiah 11:7-9; 54:13, 14) there will be peace on earth for all mankind and the animal creation; However,

At the same time we must keep in mind that there will be human beings on the earth apart from the raptured church and resurrection saints; from them, children will be born with a sinful nature. Even after perfect peace in a perfect environment, men will still not submit to the righteousness of God. The millennium will prove, once and for all, that some humans will not change even under perfect rule.

We will reign with Christ as kings and priest (1Peter 2:9) and will serve in various capacities during the millennium.

The time of the *marriage supper* in relation to the time of the tribulation period will be a time of training and preparation for reigning with Christ during the millennium. Our faithfulness to Him today will determine our responsibilities during the kingdom age. *Don't be left out in the "shame".*

3. After the Millennium (Revelation 20:7-15)

Let us consider here two (2) *finals...?*

1. The Final Battle (7-10) Satan will be loosed after being bound for a thousand years; *even after Christ has reigned a thousand years with*

perfect peace, Satan will still be able to gather a huge army (whose number is as the sand of the sea) to fight against the saints;

    a. *(v.9) Satan's armies are no match for God; fire comes down from heaven and totally destroys them;*

It is still a true saying of God:"You shall hold your peace and He (God) shall fight your battle"... for the battle is not yours... It's the Lords.

    b. (v.10) the deceiver, the Devil, Satan is captured and cast into the lake of fire, where the Beast and the false prophet are. They all are condemned eternally to torment *forever and ever.*

Author's Point: What *foul* company! Now consider that Satan despises you...do you want to be in his company forever and ever? I think not! So why not make arrangements, now, to avoid that deadly situation; accept the grace of God right now. That's the only *sane* alternative.

2. The Final Judgment (11-15)

    a. (v.1) John see a great white throne; it is so great that *all of heaven and earth flees from it; BUT, there is nowhere to run; nowhere to hide;*

    b. (John 5:22) *the judge on the throne is Christ...now He will be your Savior (attorney), then He will be your Judge;*

Author's Point: A story is told of a man who had a judgment against him and needed a lawyer to represent him. He went to one lawyer, explained his cause and asked the fee for representation. The lawyer told him he would take his case for *one thousand dollars.* The man reasoned within himself that he could get the case handled for less than that. He went to another lawyer. This lawyer's fee was *two-thousand dollars*; and subsequently to another whose fee was *three-thousand dollars.* With this he decided to go back to the first attorney for his fee was less than all. Sorrowfully, when he reentered the office of the first lawyer, things were drastically changed. The lawyer was now seated behind a huge desk...dressed in a black robe; the man asked if he would still take his case. The man responded..."*I'm sorry sir, but since you were here, things have changed; I am no longer a lawyer; I have been appointed judge.*

"This day that you hear My voice, harden not your heart..." (Psalm 95:8)

> a. (v.12) *a resurrection takes place here! John sees* **"the dead...small and great, rich and poor...standing before God"**; *Death is the common denominator for all mankind; there is no respect of persons.*

Author's Point: When I was in the military (Navy), each grade had areas that they could frequent aboard ship where lower grades could not enter. As an E-3, (non-officer), I could not enter the E-4 quarters; later as an E-4, I couldn't enter the E-5 quarters and so on...all the way up to Captain. However, after becoming a Pastor, going to Jefferson Barracks (the National Cemetery in Missouri) to do interments, I noticed an awesome thing; there was no distinction or *grade* levels in burial placements. Along the plots, there is an admiral here with a private buried next to him; a captain buried next to a NCO. *Death is the common denominator!*

Death gives up the body; *Hades* gives up the soul: It is then that the two shall be re-united.

This is not a judgment of righteous and unrighteous; (Hebrews 9:27) this is a judgment of condemnation; whosoever is to be judged is all ready condemned. The time of saints judgment is now; *(1Corinthians 11:28) ...let a man examine himself". Our sin has been condemned on the cross.*

The *Books* (v.12);

> a. (John 12:48) The Bible, *The words of Christ, will condemn those who rejected Him;*

> b. (v.15) the Book of Life; *whosoever name was not found in it was cast into the lake of fire;*

Author's Point: All persons that are born, their names are placed in the Book of Life. As Unbelievers die, their names are taken out of the book and when all have died and their names removed, the book becomes the "Lambs" Book of Life.

> c. There is also the book of the *"deeds" of man. Of course, man cannot be saved by deeds, however, God, being the righteous judge, will consider the deeds of man in punishment and in rewards.*

Author's Point: (Romans 3:19) There will be no arguments entertained from sinners; "...that every mouth may be stopped"! Can't you just imagine some sinners presenting their case? *"Wait a minute! This ain't right! Somebody made a mistake".* **(I suppose that's the only thing they are right about! Somebody did make a mistake!);** *second resurrection plus second death equals eternal hell!*

Satan and sin have been judged; human rebellion has been put down; now God will usher in the new heaven and new earth...eternal bliss for His people!

I've got a new home, Over in Zion. Its mine, mine, all mine!!!

OUR ETERNAL HOME (Revelation 21-22)

The theme of these two (2) chapters is stated in (21:5); *"...all things new!"*

The New Things

1. <u>The New Heaven and Earth</u> (Revelation 21:1,2)

    (a.) The *"former" heaven and earth have passed away; the GREEK equivalent of "new" used here* (KAINOS) *means "new in character".*

(2Peter 3:7-10) This has been a *"fiery judgment" for the purging of sin and all manner of evil.* All things shall be tried by fire.

Author's Point: The heaven and earth are new in the sense that God has removed all sin, all ungodly men and anything of the sort. Behold the earth and heavens are *"new in character"*. A new residence for a new people!

    (a) John states that there was *"no sea"* in the New Jerusalem.

Many see this as a sign that there will be a completely new and different form of water supply or; could this be a "figurative" or even spiritual translation?

Author's Point: (v6) "I will give unto him that is athirst...<u>water </u>of life freely." Could this be the reason for there being (v.2) no more sea or regular water supply? He will be the supply with eternal water of the fountain of life.

In another sense, Swete explains that since *"seas"* are dividers and are a part of the past disorder, they cannot be a part of the new order. He explains that it is at variance with the character of the New Creation. This divider of nations and *churches* has no place in a world of deathless life and unbroken peace.

2. <u>The New People of God</u> (Revelation 21:3-8)

The tabernacle of God is with men! Hallelujah, Praise God for:

    (a) He will dwell with them (us);

(b) They (we) shall be His people;

God Himself shall be with them (us), and He will be their (our) God. (*I cannot help but be "self inclusive).*

And we shall be in the land of *no more*;

> **1.** *No more* death, sorrow, crying, pain; these *former* things are passed away. The promises are *faithful and true* because they are from the *"Faithful and True Witness"*, Jesus the Christ!

All these former things; agonies, anxieties and anguish *came into the world through sin (Genesis 3). Now through Christ, they have all been eliminated and the curse removed.*   (Rev. 22:3).

> (c) (v.6) *"It is done"* parallels the saying of Christ at Calvary, *"It is finished"*; nothing is left undone; *the same that started creation will also finish it! He is Alpha and Omega; GREEK; from beginning to end, first and last;*

> (d) From the very beginning (2:7), John has referred to us as *overcomers.* Here in these final verses, he gives us *"all things" plus Son-ship! Paul declares (Galatians) that through the grace of God in Jesus Christ, we obtain son-ship and are no longer called servants.*

> *(e) v.8)* declares that many will not enter into this glory: the fearful, *cowards and unbelievers, those who could not, would not make the decision to follow Christ; those who "went along with the crowd".*

NOTE: Beware of the crowd; It was a crowd that crucified Jesus.

"I'll go, if I have to go...by myself; I'll go if I have to go, by myself.

If my mother, don't go; and my father don't go, my sister or my brother;

I'll go...If I have to go by myself.

Author's Point: Cowards, fearful; *Fear is a deceiving tactic of the adversary. Fear stunts, stills and stifles one into inactivity. So often I witness people in worship; they want to praise, they want to let go but they are afraid of what "people" will say. Not realizing that whether they do or not, people are still going to say. Trying to please people is a "never do". However, (Proverbs 16:7) when a man pleases God, even his enemies must be at peace with him. In all your "deliverance", get delivered from people! Don't be a coward.*

Author's Point: *I often think of the many that will miss this glory and their only excuse will be "I was just doing my job;" i.e.; (Lawyers, judges who defend and set known criminals free; killers for hire; fall-guys who cover for wrong-doers; "I was just doing my job", conforming to the ways of man.! As one learned prosecuting attorney puts it; "I'm not looking for the truth; I'm trying to put you away!*

Author's Note: When a man is afraid to take a stand for Christ, there is no limit to what he might do or what sin he will commit.

3. <u>The New Jerusalem</u> (Revelation 21:9-27)

John is again carried away in the Spirit; this time to a *high mountain.* There, he is shown the *New Jerusalem* coming down from heaven; we note here that the New Jerusalem is titled the same as the Church; *the Bride, the Lamb' wife.*

The *New* Jerusalem; there are two (2) GREEK words translated *new* in the NT; (1) NEOS, and the one used here, KAINOS, which has as its meaning *"fresh life rising from the decay and wreck of the old".* The scripture does not give the indication that the heavens and earth is NEOS, *"being brought into existence for the first time"*, but that they possess a *new character.*

The New Jerusalem

a. (v.10) *"...That great city, the Holy Jerusalem; descending out of heaven from God".* This is not a huge piece of "real estate" coming from the sky but rather a new attitude and atmosphere in God.

b. (v.11) *"Having the glory of God..."* like a stone most precious; like jasper, clear as crystal;

c. (vss.12, 13, 14) the wall, great and high, and the gates of the walls, with the foundations, unites the people of God from the OT, the NT Israel and the Church;

    1. (v.12) on the gates, the names of the twelve tribes of the children of Israel;

    aa. On the East three gates; on the West three gates; on the South, three gates; on the North, three gate;

(Ezekiel 48:30-53) Reuben, Judah, Levi, Joseph, Benjamin, Dan, Simeon, Issachar, Zebulon, Gad, Asher, Naphtali

    2. (v.14) the walls had twelve foundations; in them the names of the twelve Apostles of the Lamb.

    aa. Matthew, Peter, Andrew, James, John, James, the son of Alphaeus; Lebbaeus Thaddaeus, Phillip, Bartholomew, Thomas, Simon, the Canaanite; and (Acts 1:26) Matthias;

The dimensions and descriptions of the city are astounding and staggering to our imagination. As with God, any words that we can use to describe it takes away from its glory. In the word of Dr. O.K. Patterson, we simply say, *WOW!!!*

a. (v.16) the city lieth four-square; it is as long as it is wide; *"equal on all sides"; perfect; a "holy of holies" with the divine presence of God.*

    aa. Using our present table of measures, the city measure about 1500 miles in each direction, about 2/3rd the size of the United States;

Schools of thought differ as to whether the city is *cube shaped* or a pyramid. To this author, it appears to be more cubed or square; length as long a breadth; four (4) sections of (3) gates each; If pyramid, it seem more likely (3) sets of four gates; North, South, East, West.

(v.21) *"And the street of the city ... "* **The word translated for street is, (GREEK, PLATEIA) meaning a "broad place" from which we get our word** *"plaza."*

    b. (vs.18-20) the foundations are garnished with all manner of precious stones; (1Peter 4:10) a great representation of the manifold *(many colored)* grace of God;

        bb.(1) jasper (2) sapphire (3) chalcedony (4) emerald (5) sardonyx (6) sardius (7) chrysolyte (8) beryl (9) topaz (10) chrysoprasus (11) jacinth (12) amethyst. We know of no satisfactory interpretation of these colors.

    c. (v.21) the gates are pearl; the streets are pure gold; as transparent glass; on each gate, the name of one of the tribes of Israel, Sons of Jacob.

There are different lists giving the names of the *Twelve Sons of Jacob* and listings of the *Twelve Tribes of Israel.* Some names are included on one list and not included on another. The first list begins in (Genesis 29:32) with the conception of Reuben, the first born and concludes with the birth of Benjamin, (Genesis 35:18; 23-26), and *Jacob's name has been changed to Israel.*

(Genesis 29:32-35:18; 23-36, Numbers 1:5-15)

Reuben, Simeon, Levi, Judah, Dan, Naphtali, Gad, Asher, Issachar, Zebulon, Joseph, Benjamin

In (Revelation 6:5-8) 144,000, 12,000 from each of the twelve tribes of Israel are sealed: *Dan is left out; Manasseh, son of Joseph, is added.*

(Ezekiel 48:30-53) states, specifically, that the *gates of the city shall be named for the (12) tribes of Israel* and following is the list given;

Reuben, Judah, Levi, Joseph, Benjamin, Dan, Simeon, Issachar, Zebulon, Gad, Asher, Naphtali

In (Genesis 49: 3-27), Jacob gives prophetic blessings upon his sons. Some things that he prophecies are not so favorable. Yet he blesses them. This gives vent to the fact that no matter what we do, I.E., (Reuben Is unstable; went in unto his father's concubine and defiled his father's bed by so doing; Simeon and Levi were instruments of cruelty, slaying men in their anger) *grace* is powerful enough to restore and to provide blessings. It testifies of the power of God to transform character. He has the power to transform us from *"Jacobs" into "Israels". He can, and will, change your name and your character!*

Author's Point: As parents, we should be very mindful and careful what we call our children or what predictions we make concerning them. God regards what we say for we have the power of life and death in the tongue.

Also, children, regardless to what negatives are stated about you, you have the power, through God, to transform yourself into better and not be consumed in what others have to say about you.

(1Chronicles 4:9, 10) Jabez's mother *called* him *sorrow, (pain)* but Jabez *called* on the name of the Lord. Just because someone calls you a snake, does not mean you have to crawl; just because someone calls you a dog, does not mean you have to bark. You too, have the power of success and failure in your tongue. Call on the Name of the Lord and speak life!!!!

I AM WHAT GOD SAYS I AM!!!

Things there are no need of nor will there be:

1. (v.22) **temple**; since God dwells personally with His people, no temple is necessary;

2. ((v.23) **sun and moon**; the glory of God lightens the city and the Lamb is the light thereof;

3. (v.25) **night**; night represents *darkness, death sin and sorrow, none of which will be present; the gates shall never close.*

Author's Point: So many of the songs we sing are blatantly out of alignment and out of touch with scripture. The earthly analogies are understandable, however it is not canonical, i.e., "when the gates swing open, I'll walk in", (Rev. 21:25) the gates shall not be shut at all by day and there will be no night; also, "I'm going to tell the Lord when I get home how you treated me in this world"; (Revelation 21:27) Nothing that brings sorrow shall enter the city. Besides, with all that glory and the fact that "you made it", why bring up that "junk". We left that on the other side! Praise God!!!

The only ones in the city now are "they which are written in the "Lamb's Book of Life."

The Millennium

Some views regarding the millennium:

(1)Some view this as merely a spiritual condition of the redeemed and say that it cannot be given any chronological or numerical interpretation. They feel that since the book is so full of symbolisms, this is merely another symbol of fullness and completion;

(2)Some hold the strange view that the millennium has all ready taken place, relating it to the conversion of Constantine;

(3)Some say that we are now in the millennium; (God forbid; I hope not!)

(4)Many, including this author, believe that this is an actual prophecy of a thousand year period of peace following Armageddon. Christ will reign on the earth as King of kings and Lord of lords. During this period, the Church, converted Israel and the OT saints will reign with Him.

Millennial Viewpoints

A. *Postmillennialism: This view says that the millennium represents the triumph of the gospel in the period leading up to the Second Coming of Christ. In other words, the return of Christ will come **after** the millennium.*

B. *Amillennialism: Denies that there is any literal millennium or reign of Christ on earth. It is said to be only a **"spiritual reign or state of mind of the believer." If there is such a thing as a millennium, we are presently in it!***

C. *Premillenniaism: It interprets (Revelation 20) as referring to a literal reign of Christ for a literal thousand years following His second coming. The second coming occurs "before" the millennium, thus "pre" millennial. The return of Christ will initiate the millennium.*

This period marks the Christian *Sabbath*

4. The New Paradise (Revelation 22:1-5).

(Genesis 1:2) the old *heaven and earth* were plunged into chaos by Satan and sin;

In this *new* (GREEK; KAINOS) creation, God reverses *(turns around)* all the tragedies and maladies of the old creation.

a. (Genesis 2:10) In the Garden of Eden, there was an earthly river; Revelation 22:1) here in the New Jerusalem, there is a *crystal clear river.*

b. (Genesis 3:24) The *__Tree of Life__ is guarded and man is kept from it; (Revelation 22:2) the **Tree of Life** is available to the people of God;

c. (Genesis 3:14-17) The curse entered the world through sin; (Revelation 22:3) there is *no more* curse.

d. (Genesis 3:23, 24) Adam and Eve were evicted from the garden, from the face of God and commanded to toil for their daily bread; (Revelation 22:3b, 4) Here, men serve God and see Him face to face. This grants the request in *"The Lord's Prayer", "give us this day our daily bread"...*

In the first creation, man lost his kingship and became slaves; here the kingship is regained and they *reign with Christ forever!*

(v.6) "*...these sayings are faithful and true" ...* and must shortly be done.

5. The Final Message (Revelation 22:6-21)

a. (v. 7,12, 20) three times, Christ utters the words, *"I come quickly";* this is not to indicate in John's days but when these things start to occur, they will come *swiftly and without delay;*

The Final Message

Author's Point: This is a message to today's saints again to "be ye also ready…" living each day in *expectation and anticipation.*

(v.7) Beatitude: Blessed is he that keeps the sayings of the prophecy of this book.

> a. (vs. 8, 9) John bows to the angel and is rebuked. Christ, alone is to be worshipped;

> b. (Daniel 12:4) Daniel, the prophet is told to *"shut up the words and seal the book; here…* (Revelation 22:10) John is told **"seal not the sayings of the prophecy"** for the time is **"at hand".**

> c. (v.11) **"He that is unjust, let him be unjust still";** This is not an argument for sinners to remain unchanged; it is a warning that man's continued sin defines his character and determines his destiny;

(Daniel 12:10) *"The wicked shall do wickedly"* **and perform wickedness; this is a** *character* **trait. Men make their own decisions; God does not tempt man with evil (James 1:13) nor force him to righteousness (Rev. 22:15).**

(v.14) Beatitude: Blessed are they that do His commandments that they may have right to the tree of life and may enter in through the gates into the city.

(v.15) Don't be left out *"for without are dogs, sorcerers and whoremongers and murderers and idolaters and whosoever loveth and maketh a lie."*

"He, who lies down with dogs, will get up with fleas."

The final verses of this book are a plea, a promise and a prayer;

1. The plea, invitation;

    a. V.17) *COME; **him that heareth; him that is athirst; whosoever will.***

2. The promise, warning;

    a. (v.18) *If any man adds to the words of this prophecy, God shall add unto him the plagues of this book;*

    b. (v.19) *if any man shall take away from the words of this book, God shall take his part out of the book of life, and the holy city, and from the things which are written in this book.*

3. The Prayer;

"Even so, Come Lord Jesus"!

They Grace of Our Lord, Jesus Christ be with You All. *AMEN!*

Since this commentary is not exhaustive, this is NOT

The End

*The Meaning of the Tree of Life

"And out of the ground the Lord God made every tree grow that is pleasant to the sight and good for food. The tree of life was also in the midst of the garden, and the tree of the knowledge of good and evil." (Genesis 2:9).

Many schools of thought and philosophy, see the Adam and Eve story as merely a parable, an allegory or just a bit of fiction. However, believing God and the Holy Writ as I do, I believe that this story really happened. It is my feeling that if one cannot accept the "In the beginning" of the Bible, then it is of no use to reach at the "For God so loved the world…" part.

Yes, there really was an Adam and an Eve, **a Tree of Life in the garden, and the Tree of the Knowledge of Good and Evil.** But this is not the point. Information without application is no sensation… so…what we need to do is get to the significance of those trees, and understand what they represent for us today.

God told Adam not to eat from the Tree of the Knowledge of Good and Evil, along with the warning, *"for on the day that you eat of it, you will surely die"*. Here now, my position is that it becomes evident that *"they just didn't believe what God said"*. It is amazing to me how much we doubt God and give so much allegiance to what Satan or "others" might have to say concerning us. I think sometimes that we are more controlled by what Jesus (God) **didn't** say rather than what He actually said. For instance, Jesus and His disciples are in a boat headed to *"the other side"*. *On the way, the wind became boisterous and the waves contrary.* Jesus had said nothing about drowning only *"let us go over to the other side.* However, at the first sign on danger they cried out *"Master, we perish"*. They paid more attention to what He didn't say rather than what He said.

It is most apparent that Adam and Eve didn't believe what God said but allowed Satan to distract them from God's intent and purpose for them. Does this sound familiar?

Now then, there was no such prohibition concerning the Tree of Life. If Adam had eaten from that tree, *the Tree of Life*, he would have lived forever and never died. Instead he and Eve ended up eating from the forbidden tree, because they listened to a voice which tempted them to **doubt the goodness of God.**

This always has been and still is Satan's tactic even with us today. He still uses the lust of the flesh, the lust of the eyes and the pride of life and…unfortunately, it still works. We neglect the LIFE God gives and end up trying to attain it by going on a path forbidden by God. In other words, trying to get what God actually wants for us by means that are contrary to His will and way. (Romans 10:3)

What a great and significant difference it would have been if Adam had instead **chosen** to eat from the Tree of Life! God had said, "Of every tree in the garden you may freely eat..." Adam could have eaten from the Tree of Life! In doing so, he would have known God in an even greater way, and would never have died in any way! (John 11:25, 26). If he had eaten of the Tree of Life, he would never have been interested in the forbidden tree. *It is also significant that there is no record of Adam ever having eaten of the tree given to him.* Like a child, Adam (we) are more interested in what is not given us rather than what we have right to. Having NEGLECTED or chose not to partake of the Right tree, it was really only a matter of time before he would fall to the temptation of eating the forbidden fruit.

Too many times we get into trouble because we focus on the forbidden thing. We fight with temptation, and lose, because we focus on the temptation. God wants us to get our eyes off the temptation, and even off the moral rules of what would be right and wrong, so we can get our eyes onto what He wants us to focus on. It is of a truth that we inevitably move towards our most dominant thought. (Luke 12:34).

So here now, what does the Tree of Life represent? I believe it represents Jesus, the **source of Life!** Jesus said, "I am the Way, the Truth and the LIFE, no one comes to the Father but by Me!" (John 14:6). The gift of Jesus that is available to us represents far more than the forgiveness of sins. It represents the very life of God by which we can truly live abundantly! The whole truth then is to focus on Jesus (the Tree of Life) and not to be *distracted* by lesser concerns (selfish knowledge and personal agendas) even the concern of "is this good or is this evil?" If we learn to focus on Jesus, we will tap into the unlimited source of life, power, joy and strength that we need to be "more than conquerors" in this life.

When we truly "eat" enough of that tree, of Jesus, we will live forever. Sin in some form will always look attractive to us unless we get a new focus. We must focus on Jesus; we must learn to see things through God's eyes: we must focus on His glory and goodness. He alone is to be worshipped. (Revelation 22:9). It is impossible to focus on more than one thing at a time. No man can serve two or multiple gods. (Matthew 6:24).

If we continue to focus on the *Tree of Life, Jesus,* and eat and drink of His treasure, we will come to know Him in the power of His resurrection that leads us to *eternal life.*

Good change doesn't happen when we focus on ourselves. This might be a surprise to some readers. But it is true. Satan loves to get us to look to ourselves. So many young folk are going around today "*looking for themselves.*" What they don't realize is that if they can find themselves, they will have only found disappointment, distress and dismay for there is no victory in self. A sure mark of a satanic religion is one that tells you to look inside yourself for the answer.

There are many variations on this theme. One is the eastern meditation type thing, where you are told to get in touch with your own godhood.

Right here I think I ought to warn you to beware of the **Gospel of Oprah!** (which in effect is more gossip than gospel.) However, Oprah's theory is that Jesus is not the only way to God, just one way among many. She also maintains that *we are all gods and all we must do is look inside ourselves and make contact with this god in us.* WOW! Look inside us among the "*wickedness of man...and every imagination of the thoughts of his heart are evil continually (Genesis 6:5) and find a god?* **Get real! That's not the answer!**

There is another variation, far more subtle, and far more likely to appeal to Christians. That is, to measure yourself up against certain moral or spiritual principles, and consider how well or badly you are doing, and resolving to improve, you know, like a New Years resolution. Multitudes of sincere people are doing this, and fail to realize that in this way they will never become what God wants them to be. Looking at self is a fruit of eating from the Tree of the Knowledge of Good and Evil. Listen, just knowing good and evil doesn't give you the power to do what is right, however. Knowing what to do doesn't give you the power to do it.

When Adam and Eve ate of the forbidden tree, they began to be self-conscious. They started looking at themselves and became ashamed. They knew they were naked. Until then, they weren't even aware of that. I kind of think they were covered with somewhat of a *garment of praise and worship to the God of all creation!* Covered thusly, they lived in the presence of Almighty God without shame. (Have you ever thought; mankind is the only creature of God that wears clothes to cover)?

After eating of the forbidden Tree, they lost that glorious covering and began to be selfish and desire to escape from the presence of Almighty God. The problem with looking at yourself and your problems is that you inevitably end up focusing on the evil within you. It is a law of the mind that whatever you primarily focus on ends up dominating your life. It's very important that Jesus has Lordship over the imaginations of our heart.

Satan is doing all he can to oppose this, using such means as television, video games, unclean music, false teachers and religions, personal ambition, lying philosophies ... the list goes on and on. If Jesus doesn't have a major part of your imagination, something else does, and it works to make you fall short of the glory of God. (Romans 3:23) No one ever became holy or better simply by seeing their weaknesses and resolving to change in their own power. No, the answer is still to go back to the Tree of Life, to Jesus. Adam and Eve lost this opportunity, but we regained it because Jesus Himself paid for all our sins at the cross, on a tree, making for us the way to return to true God consciousness.

If you look at yourself, judging yourself by your knowledge of good and evil, you will either end up congratulating yourself for your good performance (self-righteousness) or becoming depressed because of the guilt of failing to live up to those standards. Neither of these results is what God wants. God made us for Him, and He is not satisfied when we prefer to ignore Him and become wrapped up in our own righteousness or lack thereof. He wants us to enjoy Him, to trust Him, and that only happens when we dare to take our eyes off of self, and trust the power of His cross, and begin to get our eyes on Him.

How to Get Your Eyes off self and on Jesus

Attitude is very important here. God requires an attitude of faith. True faith comes through the recognition of Jesus. This knowledge of Jesus can come to us through anointed preaching and teaching of God's Word, through times of worship, through the direct action of the Holy Spirit enlightening us, through the study of the Bible, or through seeing Christ in a true Christian.

In each case we have to see beyond the means God uses to reveal Christ to us; we have to see Jesus Himself. We must not give our hearts to the methods and forget who it is about.

If we focus on methods, even methods of Bible study, praise and worship, or anointed preachers, we once again fall short of the mark, and end up turning to the Tree of the Knowledge of Good and Evil, rather than to the Tree of Life.

You have to know and accept that *it's not about you! It all about He who was crucified, on a tree; laid in a tomb... and arose on Resurrection Day with all power in His hand...and allow me to say...power with the authority to use it! JESUS IS THE TREE OF LIFE. EAT THEREOF!!!*

Make Jesus your passion, and you will change. Don't be distracted by anything. Don't even allow yourself to focus on the ways God could bless you. Trust that in everything He brings you to, there is a way to see Jesus. Then your faith will grow strong, and more than that, you will be filled with the life of God Himself. This is the true fountain of satisfaction for the soul of man. Accept no substitutes!

Bibliography

THE HOLY BIBLE; NKJV; ERV; KJV;

Swete, Henry Barclay. *The apocalypse of St. John.*

Wiersby, Warren J.; Commentary *on the Old and New Testament.*

The Commentator's Commentary; *Revelation*, Earl F. Palmer.

The Wycliffe Bible Commentary; Pfeiffer and Harrison;

      Wilbur Smith, D.D.; Professor of English Bible, Fuller Theological Seminary, Pasadena, CA.

H. H. Halley's Bible Handbook, *Deluxe Edition, with the NIV, Revision 2000; 2007*

G. H. Pember

Abbreviations:

NKJV	*New King James Version*
ERV	*English Revised Version*
KJV	*King James Version*
OT	*Old Testament*
NT	*New Testament*
NIV	*New International Version*

Books of the Bible (abbreviations)

OT; Gen Ex Lev Num Deut Josh Jud Ruth ISam IISam IKngs IIKngs IChron IIChron Ezr Neh Est Job Ps Prov Eccl Song Isa Jer Lam Eze Dan Hos Joel Amos Obad Jon Mic Nah Hab Zeph Hag Zech Mal

NT: Matt Mark Luke John Acts Rom ICor IICor Gal Eph Phil Col IThess IIThess ITim IITim Titus Philm Heb Jas IPet IIPet IJn IIJn IIIJn Jude Rev

About the author

Steven G. Thompson is senior pastor/teacher at the historic Leonard Missionary Baptist church of St. Louis, Missouri. After serving as moderator for four years, he is now *Moderator Emeritus* of the Antioch District Missionary Baptist Association also in Saint Louis.

In 1999, under Dr. Thompson's leadership, Leonard Baptist Church began worship in its new edifice and continues to grow and glow in outreach and evangelism.

An accomplished author and playwright, he has written several books and is a highly sought speaker, evangelist and counselor. He has served as presenter/instructor in local and state congresses of the National Baptist Convention, U. S. A., Inc. and the Missionary Baptist State Convention of Missouri. He has served as lecturer for several auxiliaries of the local, state and national auxiliaries of this convention.

Rev. Thompson is an award-winning gospel radio announcer and has received numerous awards in that field. He is also a member of the board of directors for the Western Baptist Bible College in Kansas City, Missouri, the St. Louis Clergy Coalition, and the Minister's Union of Saint Louis and vicinity.

Dr. Thompson is a proud *"bulldog" and member of the alumni association for the historic Sumner High School in Saint Louis.*

In 1993, Thompson received a Bachelor of Arts degree from Glad Tidings Bible College; and in 2004, he received a Master of Divinity degree from Claremont University. Most recently, he received a Doctorate of Divinity degree from Claremont University.

To his honor, in August of 2008, *"School"* Street, intersecting Compton Avenue, between Dr. Martin Luther King Drive and Barack Obama Boulevard was *"renamed" "Rev. Steven G. Thompson Drive"*...to God be the glory!

A native of Luxora, Arkansas, Rev. Thompson is a husband *(Merlean),* father, and grandfather.

Revelation Refresher

1. How many chapters are in the Book of Revelation
   a. 20
   b. 21
   c. 22
   d. 23
2. The writer of this great book of Revelation is;
   a. John *the* Baptist
   b. John Mark
   c. "I" John
   d. John *the Apostle*
3. The ways in which we interpret scripture are
   a. Literal, formative, prospective
   b. Figurative, parenthetically, prophetic
   c. Perspective, liturgical, purposefully
   d. Figurative, prophetic, literal
4. We are told through study that the book was written around 95 A.D.; A.D. is a abbreviation for;
   a. Augustus Dominus
   b. Anno-Domini
   c. After-Death
   d. Anti-Diluvium
5. Besides the Book of Revelation, this author is further given credit for penning
   a. The Gospel of Jonah, 1st 2nd & 3rd Judas, Ruth
   b. The Gospel of John, 1st, 2nd, 3rd John
   c. The Book of Acts, and the Gospel of Luke
   d. All of the Epistles of Paul
6. The Book of Revelation is a *mystery* rather than a problem. Because of this, its meanings must be
   a. Decided rather than denied
   b. Dedicated rather than Destined
   c. Convicted rather than Committed
   d. Revealed rather than solved.

7. Christ told the author, *"what you see, write it in a book and send it to*
    a. All Churches for all times
    b. The Seven Churches at Asia Minor
    c. The Sixteen Churches in the Vatican
    d. The Seven Churches at Australia Major

8. In (v.8) of the first chapter, Jesus refers to Himself as *Alpha and Omega.* This is reference to the GREEK as
    a. In the Beginning was the Word
    b. First and last letter of the alphabet
    c. Almighty and Omni-Present
    d. Almost on the Other side

9. Which of these is not one of the Churches addressed?
    a. Philadelphia
    b. Sardis
    c. Pamphilia
    d. Ephesus
    e. Laodicea

10. In Chapter one, verse sixteen; the writer saw *one like unto the Son of Man* having seven (7) stars in His right hand. The Stars represent
    a. The Angels of the Churches
    b. The Messengers of the Churches
    c. The Pastor's of the Churches
    d. All of the above
    e. None of the above

11. The text reveals to us that when John saw the Christ,
    a. He ran to Him, fell on His neck and kissed Him
    b. He fled from His presence
    c. He cried out in fear
    d. He fell at His feet
    e. He ask Him His name

12. True_____ False _____ The *Seven Candlesticks* of the book represent the Seven Spirits around the throne of God.

13. True _____ False _____ Two Words that were prominent in the message to each church are *"I Know".*

14. How many books are there in the Holy Bible?
    a. 22
    b. 33
    c. 55
    d. 66
15. How many "resurrections" are there as mentioned in the Book of Revelation?
    a. One
    b. Two
    c. Three
    d. Four
    e. Five
16. What are the groups taking part in the first resurrection?
    a. OT- Saints, Tribulation Saints and the Church
    b. Rejuvenated Israel
    c. New Orleans Saints and St. Louis Rams
    d. None of the above
    e. All of the Above
17. Which of the following is **not one** of the views concerning the interpretation of the millennium?
    a. AnnoMillennialism
    b. Amillennialism
    c. PreMillennialism
    d. PostMillennialism
18. First Thessalonians chapter 4 verses 13-17 describes
    a. The conversion of John the Baptist
    b. The taking away of the Church to be with the Lord
    c. The destruction of Gog and Magog
    d. John on the Isle of Patmos
19. The GREEK word KAINOS has as its English translation meaning
    a. The art and Science of Scriptural alignment
    b. The transformation word "And".
    c. New in character
    d. New as in never before in existence
    e. NEOS

20. For the Word of God and the testimony of the Lord, John was cast on an Isle called
    a. Philadelphia
    b. Pergamos
    c. Crete
    d. Patmos
    e. Phylactery

21. John saw the glorified Christ in the midst of seven (7) golden lampstands. The lampstands represented
    a. The seven (7) spirits mentioned in Isaiah 11
    b. The Seven days of the calendar week
    c. Seven Pastors (messengers)
    d. Seven Churches

22. When John was commanded to *"come up here", we reasoned that this was a "symbol"* of
    a. A command to move
    b. The Rapture of the church
    c. A summons to preach in the seven churches
    d. PostMillenial Trauma

23. "Know you not that your body is the *"TEMPLE"* of the Holy ghost" ; "Behold the *"Tabernacle"* of God is with men." The Temple is
    a. Man Made
    b. Mobile
    c. Make believe
    d. Symbolic
    e. Stationary

24. After the Millennium comes the
    a. First Resurrection
    b. Second Resurrection
    c. Resurrection of the tribulation Saints
    d. Battle of Armageddon

25. The Battle of Armageddon will be fought on a "natural" battle field called
    a. Armagedd
    b. Memphis
    c. Megiddo
    d. Mega-Dominion

26. The GREEK word KAI means
    a. New in character
    b. And
    c. Also
    d. About
    e. Anno-Domini

27. We hold the truth in the theory that the arrangement of the City of New Jerusalem is "square" in configuration. The alternate theory if that the city is shaped like a
    a. Circle
    b. Pyramid
    c. Obtuse Angle
    d. Hexagon

28. Another name for the Great White Throne Judgment is the
    a. Bema Seat Judgment
    b. Judgment of the Two Witnesses
    c. Fulfillment of Hades
    d. Coming together of body and soul

29. Through study, we found that there are essentially four *"kinds"* of churches. They are
    a. Baptist, Catholic, C.O.G.I.C, and Methodist
    b. Admonitory, Prophetic, Local and Legal
    c. Sanctified, Holiness, Missionary and Logistic
    d. Prophetic, Local, Personal and Admonitory

30. Two of the Seven Churches received no "accusation"; they are
    a. Sardis and Smyrna
    b. Thyatira and Laodicea
    c. Philadelphia and Pergamos
    d. Smyrna and Philadelphia

31. One of the seven churches received no approval. That Church was
    a. Laodicea
    b. Smyrna
    c. Ephesus
    d. Thyatira

32. Another word for the *Bottomless Pit* or the *abode of Demons* is
    a. Alcatraz
    b. Abomination
    c. Abyss
    d. Abstract Domain
33. The army of locust is loosed from the abode of Demons and will do their job for a period of
    a. 150 years
    b. Six months
    c. 150 days
    d. Seven Days
34. The souls "under the altar" that pray the prayer *"how long"* are praying for
    a. Victory
    b. Venom
    c. Vengeance or revenge
    d. Vindication
35. In the opening of the "seven seals, how many of the seals produced horse riders?
    a. One
    b. Two
    c. Three
    d. Four
    e. Seven
36. Jesus Christ is Our Redeemer. What of the following is **not** one of the qualifications of a redeemer?
    a. Willingness
    b. Ability
    c. Self-sacrifice
    d. Kinship
37. When the angels showed John the City of New Jerusalem, the city sat of
    a. Twelve angels who had twelve swords
    b. Twelve foundations with a great wall with twelve gates
    c. Twenty four Elders
    d. A Sea of Chrystal clear glass

38. Chapter eighteen (18) deals with three phases of Babylon, the Great Whore and her "daughters". These are
    a. Literal, figurative and prophetic
    b. Babylon, Sardis and Magog
    c. Political, Economic and Religious
    d. Northern, Western and Southern
39. Fill in the blanks: Everyone who is born into the world, their _____ is placed in the _____ of _____. As _____ die, their name is removed and the _____ becomes the _____.
40. In His earthly ministry, Jesus did not operate as the Son of God. He *"poured Himself out"* of His deity. The GREEK word for this act is
    a. REDEEMER
    b. KAINOS
    c. PHARMAKIA
    d. KENOSIS
41. The powers of the two witnesses who prophecy during the tribulation seem to identify them with
    a. Moses and Joseph
    b. Isaiah and Jeremiah
    c. Enoch and Elijah
    d. Moses and Elijah
42. At the *mid-Point of the Tribulation* a startling event will take place. It is
    a. The Rapture
    b. The revealing of the Lamb of God
    c. The revealing of the Anti-Christ
    d. The revealing of the Roman Catholic Priest
43. There are two (2) great suppers mentioned in the Book of Revelation. They are the
    a. Marriage Supper and the supper of the great gods
    b. Lord's Supper and the Lambs Supper
    c. Last Supper and First Supper
    d. Kings supper and Queens supper

44. The Penman of the Book of Revelation is
    a. John the Baptist
    b. John Mark
    c. The Brother of James
    d. The writer of the Book of Acts
    e. I John
45. Hermeneutics is defined as the
    a. Art and science of Sermon Preparation
    b. Art and Science of Scriptural interpretation
    c. Activity and Scientology
    d. GREEK politics

BONUS QUESTIONS

46. Define Exegesis:

47. Define the Theory of Pre-Millennialism:

48. Define Eisegesis:

49. Define the theory of A-millennialism:

50. Define the theory of Post-millennialism:

Revelation Refresher Answer Key

1. How many chapters are in the Book of Revelation
   a. 20
   b. 21
   c. 22
   d. 23
2. The writer of this great book of Revelation is;
   a. John *the* Baptist
   b. John Mark
   c. "I" John
   d. John *the Apostle*
3. The ways in which we interpret scripture are
   a. Literal, formative, prospective
   b. Figurative, parenthetically, prophetic
   c. Perspective, liturgical, purposefully
   d. Figurative, prophetic, literal
4. We are told through study that the book was written around 95 A.D.; A.D. is a abbreviation for;
   a. Augustus Dominus
   b. Anno-Domini
   c. After-Death
   d. Anti-Diluvium
5. Besides the Book of Revelation, this author is further given credit for penning
   a. The Gospel of Jonah, 1st 2nd & 3rd Judas, Ruth
   b. The Gospel of John, 1st, 2nd, 3rd John
   c. The Book of Acts, and the Gospel of Luke
   d. All of the Epistles of Paul
6. The Book of Revelation is a *mystery* rather than a problem. Because of this, its meanings must be
   a. Decided rather than denied
   b. Dedicated rather than Destined
   c. Convicted rather than Committed
   d. Revealed rather than solved.

7. Christ told the author, *"what you see, write it in a book and send it to*
   a. All Churches for all times
   b. The Seven Churches at Asia Minor
   c. The Sixteen Churches in the Vatican
   d. The Seven Churches at Australia Major
8. In (v.8) of the first chapter, Jesus refers to Himself as *Alpha and Omega.* This is reference to the GREEK as
   a. In the Beginning was the Word
   b. First and last letter of the alphabet
   c. Almighty and Omni-Present
   d. Almost on the Other side
9. Which of these is not one of the Churches addressed?
   a. Philadelphia
   b. Sardis
   c. Pamphilia
   d. Ephesus
   e. Laodicea
10. In Chapter one, verse sixteen; the writer saw *one like unto the Son of Man* having seven (7) stars in His right hand. The Stars represent
    a. The Angels of the Churches
    b. The Messengers of the Churches
    c. The Pastor's of the Churches
    d. All of the above
    e. None of the above
11. The text reveals to us that when John saw the Christ,
    a. He ran to Him, fell on His neck and kissed Him
    b. He fled from His presence
    c. He cried out in fear
    d. He fell at His feet
    e. He ask Him His name
12. True_____ False __x___ The *Seven Candlesticks* of the book represent the Seven Spirits around the throne of God.

13. True __x__ False _____ Two Words that were prominent in the message to each church are *"I Know".*

14. How many books are there in the Holy Bible?
   a. 22
   b. 33
   c. 55
   d. 66
15. How many "resurrections" are there as mentioned in the Book of Revelation?
   a. One
   b. Two
   c. Three
   d. Four
   e. Five
16. What are the groups taking part in the first resurrection?
   a. OT- Saints, Tribulation Saints and the Church
   b. Rejuvenated Israel
   c. New Orleans Saints and St. Louis Rams
   d. None of the above
   e. All of the Above
17. Which of the following is *not* **one** of the views concerning the interpretation of the millennium?
   a. AnnoMillennialism
   b. Amillennialism
   c. PreMillennialism
   d. PostMillennialism
18. First Thessalonians chapter 4 verses 13-17 describes
   a. The conversion of John the Baptist
   b. The taking away of the Church to be with the Lord
   c. The destruction of Gog and Magog
   d. John on the Isle of Patmos
19. The GREEK word KAINOS has as its English translation meaning
   a. The art and Science of Scriptural alignment
   b. The transformation word "And".
   c. New in character
   d. New as in never before in existence
   e. NEOS

20. For the Word of God and the testimony of the Lord, John was cast on an Isle called
    a. Philadelphia
    b. Pergamos
    c. Crete
    d. Patmos
    e. Phylactery

21. John saw the glorified Christ in the midst of seven (7) golden lampstands. The lampstands represented
    a. The seven (7) spirits mentioned in Isaiah 11
    b. The Seven days of the calendar week
    c. Seven Pastors (messengers)
    d. Seven Churches

22. When John was commanded to *"come up here", we reasoned that this was a "symbol"* of
    a. A command to move
    b. The Rapture of the church
    c. A summons to preach in the seven churches
    d. Postmillennial Trauma

23. "Know you not that your body is the *"TEMPLE"* of the Holy ghost" ; "Behold the *"Tabernacle"* of God is with men." The Temple is
    a. Man Made
    b. Mobile
    c. Make believe
    d. Symbolic
    e. Stationary

24. After the Millennium comes the
    a. First Resurrection
    b. Second Resurrection
    c. Resurrection of the tribulation Saints
    d. Battle of Armageddon

25. The Battle of Armageddon will be fought on a "natural" battle field called
    a. Armageddos
    b. Memphis
    c. Megiddo
    d. Mega-Dominion

26. The GREEK word KAI means
    a. New in character
    b. And
    c. Also
    d. About
    e. Anno-Domini
27. We hold the truth in the theory that the arrangement of the City of New Jerusalem is "square" in configuration. The alternate theory if that the city is shaped like a
    a. Circle
    b. Pyramid
    c. Obtuse Angle
    d. Hexagon
28. Another name for the Great White Throne Judgment is the
    a. Bema Seat Judgment
    b. Judgment of the Two Witnesses
    c. Fulfillment of Hades
    d. Coming together of body and soul
29. Through study, we found that there are essentially four *"kinds"* of churches. They are
    a. Baptist, Catholic, C.O.G.I.C, and Methodist
    b. Admonitory, Prophetic, Local and Legal
    c. Sanctified, Holiness, Missionary and Logistic
    d. Prophetic, Local, Personal and Admonitory
30. Two of the Seven Churches received no "accusation"; they are
    a. Sardis and Smyrna
    b. Thyatira and Laodicea
    c. Philadelphia and Pergamum
    d. Smyrna and Philadelphia
31. One of the seven churches received no approval. That Church was
    a. Laodicea
    b. Smyrna
    c. Ephesus
    d. Thyatira

32. Another word for the *Bottomless Pit* or the *abode of Demons* is
    a. Alcatraz
    b. Abomination
    c. Abyss
    d. Abstract Domain
33. The army of locust is loosed from the abode of Demons and will do their job for a period of
    a. 150 years
    b. Six months
    c. 150 days
    d. Seven Days
34. The souls "under the altar" that pray the prayer *"how long"* are praying for
    a. Victory
    b. Venom
    c. Vengeance or revenge
    d. Vindication
35. In the opening of the "seven seals, how many of the seals produced horse riders?
    a. One
    b. Two
    c. Three
    d. Four
    e. Seven
36. Jesus Christ is Our Redeemer. What of the following is **not** one of the qualifications of a redeemer?
    a. Willingness
    b. Ability
    c. Self-sacrifice
    d. Kinship
37. When the angels showed John the City of New Jerusalem, the city sat of
    a. Twelve angels who had twelve swords
    b. Twelve foundations with a great wall with twelve gates
    c. Twenty four Elders
    d. A Sea of Chrystal clear glass

38. Chapter eighteen (18) deals with three phases of Babylon, the Great Whore and her "daughters". These are
    a. Literal, figurative and prophetic
    b. Babylon, Sardis and Magog
    c. Political, Economic and Religious
    d. Northern, Western and Southern
39. Fill in the blanks: Everyone who is born into the world, their **name** is placed in the **book** of **life**. As **unbelievers** die, their name is removed and the **book** becomes the **Lambs Book of Life.**
40. In His earthly ministry, Jesus did not operate as the Son of God. He *"poured Himself out"* of His deity. The GREEK word for this act is
    a. REDEEMER
    b. KAINOS
    c. PHARMAKIA
    d. KENOSIS
41. The powers of the two witnesses who prophecy during the tribulation seem to identify them with
    a. Moses and Joseph
    b. Isaiah and Jeremiah
    c. Enoch and Elijah
    d. Moses and Elijah
42. At the *mid-Point of the Tribulation* a startling event will take place. It is
    a. The Rapture
    b. The revealing of the Lamb of God
    c. The revealing of the Anti-Christ
    d. The revealing of the Roman Catholic Priest
43. There are two (2) great suppers mentioned in the Book of Revelation. They are the
    a. Marriage Supper and the supper of the great gods
    b. Lord's Supper and the Lambs Supper
    c. Last Supper and First Supper
    d. Kings supper and Queens supper

44. The Penman of the Book of Revelation is
    a. John the Baptist
    b. John Mark
    c. The Brother of James
    d. The writer of the Book of Acts
    e. "I" John

45. Hermeneutics is defined as the
    a. Art and science of Sermon Preparation
    b. Art and Science of Scriptural interpretation
    c. Activity and Scientology
    d. GREEK politics

BONUS QUESTIONS

46. Define "biblical" Exegesis: **The art of extracting from the scripture its true (meant/intended) meaning.**

47. Define the Theory of Pre-Millennialism: **Assumes the return of Christ will occur before the millennium.**

48. Define (biblical) Eisegesis: **Reading into scripture one's assumed meaning.**

49. Define the theory of A-millennialism: **There is no literal millennium or thousand year reign of Christ and if there is, we are in it now.**

50. Define the theory of Post-millennialism: **The return of Christ will occur after the millennium.**